WAR STORIES

Spiritual Warfare & the Toxic Narratives that Sabotage Your Life

PATRICK MEYERS

Kris + Jim,

I hope you enjoy this book. It's born out of my own journey, my own experiences. I try to relay my own understanding of spiritual warfare in a practical and down to earth way. Most people are surprised to see how pervasive these issues are and how often their thoughts work against them. I hope you find something in these pages that helps you live a fuller and freer life. Blessings!

— Patrick Meyers —

VECTOR

Spiritual Direction & Transformation

Endorsements

"Dear reader, I am glad you picked up this book! I think you will be gratefully surprised. Patrick covers the subject of spiritual warfare in a way no book has before. This foundational work will illuminate truth and help you live out God's narrative for your life."

Shelley Johnson,
Founder & Director of Segullah Ministries

"This is a powerful read. Thank you, Patrick, for your living witness to this truth as it has been revealed in your life, and in the lives of so many others who you are helping escape horrific spiritual warfare and make the life-changing journey to joy."

Carlo Walth
Professor at William Jessup University,
and Director of Mentoring Sacred Arts

"I had trouble putting this book down! War Stories paints a vivid and accurate picture of the spiritual battle that we are all engaged in but seldom recognize."

Jeff Lenberg
CTO of World Light Power LLC
and World Light Africa Ltd.

"This book is a wake-up call for those of us who are sleep-walking through an ongoing battle for our hearts. Patrick offers sane, biblical, and wise instruction to equip us to defeat the attacks from the enemy of our souls. Thanks be to God!"

Dr. Howard Baker
Assistant Professor of Christian Formation
at Denver Seminary

"Patrick Meyers' work is a well-written and accessible introduction to the topic of spiritual warfare. Meyers uses engaging stories to share practical tips drawn from his unique experience. This book will deepen your awareness of the spiritual and encourage you to cling to the Lord."

Eric Nevins
Host of the podcast *Halfway There*,
and founder of Christian Podcasters Association

"This book will change your perceptions about spiritual warfare. It will open your eyes to the frontline battle ground within your own heart and the war of God's truth vs. Satan's propaganda. This book will confront, inspire, and empower anyone bold enough to read it."

Steve Forney
Spiritual Director with Soul Care Professionals

Contents

Dedication

I dedicate this book to my boys.

Sons, I am sure you know by now that life isn't always easy. Along with its many adventures and joys, it is also fraught with real dangers.

Though you were born into a world at war, I want you to know that you are more than capable of battle. I bless your warrior hearts.

> *My sons, you were born to battle; destined to overcome.*
> *Stay steadfast in your faith. Trust that you can meet any*
>   *challenge that comes your way. I have complete confidence in*
>   *your abilities. I trust your hearts.*
> *I bless you to always live boldly, and I pray that you always live*
>   *with equal measures of joy and purpose.*

Now, rise up mighty warriors, and fight for your destiny!

Dedication to the Reader

I also dedicate this to my readers.

Sadly, I know that many of you don't have fathers who will bless you or encourage you to fight spiritual battles. If that is your story, I would like to dedicate this book to you, too.

My heart aches to see you reclaim any area of your life that has been stolen, and to take your place in this battle. So, I offer you my blessing:

> *I bless you to live boldly, to fight bravely, to know your beauty, to*
> *find your strength.*
> *Child of God, know that your Heavenly Father welcomes you.*
> *He is a mighty warrior. A glorious warrior-king.*
> *The Lord beckons you to join Him as He fights to bring justice,*
> *to right wrongs, and to heal broken hearts.*
> *I welcome you to take your place alongside the armies of heaven.*
> *Know that we are stronger for having you in our ranks.*

Now, rise up mighty warriors, and fight for your destiny!

Disclaimer

This book is NOT intended as a substitute for medical or mental health advice. You should consult your doctor or a qualified mental health provider with respect to any symptoms that may require diagnosis or treatment.

This book is intended for spiritual education and edification. While I sincerely hope this book is helpful for you, I do not promise any particular outcome. No guarantees are expressed or implied. You alone are responsible for how you choose to use this information. Neither I, Patrick Meyers, nor Vector Ministries LLC, shall be liable for any physical, psychological, emotional, mental, spiritual, financial, or other damages, loss, or disruption. You are responsible for your own actions, choices, and the results that follow.

This book is a kind of memoir, a collection of reflections on my experiences with spiritual warfare. The conversations I have written come from my own recollections. Though they aren't word-for-word transcripts, the dialogue is retold in a way that accurately represents the feeling and meaning of each original conversation. I have changed each person's name in order to preserve their privacy and anonymity (after all, they have their own stories to tell).

WAR STORIES

Fight the good fight of the faith. Take hold of the eternal life to which you were called.

— 1 Timothy 6:12 —

Introduction

I wrote this book to help the Church.

I dedicated my life to helping my brothers and sisters in Christ, and I love this work. It is immensely satisfying. Yet, when I look around at the lives of those I know, of those I love, and at my own life, I can't help but see a tremendous problem.

The enemy has robbed us. All of us. Every last one of us.

Even worse, few of us seem to notice. We assume that all of the problems we have are just the way it is. We blame ourselves. Worse yet, we often blame God.

But God isn't the one who robbed us. He doesn't steal. He gives. God gives good gifts (Matt. 7:11) and He has good plans for our lives (Jer. 29:11). He dreams up ways to interact with us, touch our lives, and make things better for us. For all of us. For every last one of us.

Yet, as you surely know by now, the good life hardly comes handed to us on a silver platter. Life is hard. Unfair. Sometimes cruel.

Why? Because we live in a world at war. We have an actual enemy, a malevolent, intelligent being hellbent on destroying our destiny and sabotaging us before we ever launch.

Like ancient Israel before us, God has an inheritance to give us. The Promised Land lies before us; the life that God dreams for us. And like our spiritual ancestors, we too must fight for it.

I wrote this book to help bring the people of God a better understanding of spiritual warfare. While many of us understand the concept on a theological level, most of us need help on a practical level. And we all need a little more encouragement to keep fighting the good fight in all our battles.

That is where this book comes in. I share actual examples of spiritual warfare to illustrate what it looks like in real life. My aim is to expose the enemy's tactics and equip you to fight back.

Spiritual warfare is more than a concept. It is a reality. A daily reality. The battles we face often happen within our own hearts and minds. This is because spiritual warfare is primarily a battle of propaganda, a battle of conflicting stories that shape our lives.

Propaganda plagues us. Everywhere we turn, we are bombarded by biased information meant to persuade us to a particular point of view. We are caught in the conflict of competing narratives. From left to right, everyone seems to have a different version of the truth, a new spin on the facts, or a slanted way to interpret statistics. It often seems impossible to know what is true.

While our age is riddled with slanted narratives, this biased storytelling is nothing new. It has always been a problem—the problem. Since the dawn of human history, our enemy set out to pollute our minds with a narrative that runs contrary to the truth. Opposing the story God told, the devil tricked Adam and Eve into believing a lie. He has been lying to humanity ever since.

The devil's deceptions are strategic attacks designed to mislead us. He knows that if we fall prey to his toxic narratives, he can rob us of the life that God desires for us. Violence frequently erupts at the point where two incompatible narratives collide. It is that way in life, and it is the same with spiritual warfare. God's kingdom suffers violent attacks as evil constantly threatens the good plans God has for our lives (Matt. 11:12).

If we allow it to continue unchecked, Satan's seditious subterfuge will steal everything good from our lives. The way we counter the evil lies is by listening to the voice of truth. We must choose to believe the story God is telling.

Spiritual battles are fought with truth. Our fiercest battles happen precisely where we have believed the enemy's lies. All spiritual battles boil down to one simple question. We must each ask ourselves, *"Whose story do I want to believe?"*

ONE

The Devil & Fly-Fishing

To live in ignorance of spiritual warfare is the most naive and dangerous thing a person can do… you don't escape spiritual warfare simply because you choose not to believe it exists or because you refuse to fight it.

John Eldredge

Stay alert! Watch out for your great enemy, the devil. He prowls around like a roaring lion, looking for someone to devour.

1 Peter 5:8 NLT

I'VE HAD A LOT OF TROUBLE LATELY.

Since I started writing this book, trouble has sprung up everywhere. For starters, there is an unprecedented pandemic —which has thrown the whole world into turmoil. It seems to have shifted everything concerning how we live life. Then, here in the United States, the heated political tension has given way to racial tensions. In the wake of terrible injustice, riots have broken out across the country.

We are living in tumultuous times; times of upheaval. It seems like trouble is springing up everywhere.

Closer to home, in the last month, everything seemed to break. First, our dryer went out. Then our central air conditioning stopped working. Next, my car's brakes. After that, my car's clutch "exploded." That was the mechanic's exact word; he said my clutch *exploded*. I didn't even know that was possible. It left me stranded on the side of the interstate for a couple of hours while I waited for a tow truck.

That same week, a water pipe burst and flooded the church my office is in. The damage was incredible and affected the entire building. It left a couple inches of standing water covering the sanctuary floor. I haven't been able to use my office since. Honestly, I am not sure I will even be able to use the space again.

I have also experienced a ton of mysterious tech issues lately. One minute everything was working fine. Then out of nowhere, my phone, computer, internet, or whatever would fail. Important calls got dropped. Online meetings crashed. Later, things would go back to working as normal, yet it was never clear what had caused the problems.

On a personal note, I struggled with some intense bouts of discouragement. They hit me like tidal waves. Sometimes I felt like I would drown in their storms. It has been an arduous task to keep writing this book, to press forward and move this project along.

Tragically, since I started writing, two friends of our family committed suicide. Both men were Christians; one was even a pastor. They left behind wives, children, and lots of confused friends who now grieve their loss.

Then, as if to top it all off, I had a falling out with a good friend of mine. It was a bizarre misunderstanding that seemed to come out of nowhere. I fear that it may have damaged, or even ended, our friendship.

We had other things happen as well. We had to get major

repairs for our other car, the air conditioning went out again (and then again), and several other random things suddenly needed repair. There is a long list of issues that have happened since I started writing this book. So, like I said, life has been a little crazy filled with all this trouble.

Fish Stories

While Satan probably played a part in some of these troubles, I can't blame everything on spiritual warfare. Life can be pretty tough even without the devil's interference. After all, Jesus warned us, "in this world you will have trouble" (John 16:33).

I may never know how many of my recent troubles were truly spiritual warfare and how many were just the normal challenges of life. However, I do know that one specific experience definitely involved spiritual warfare. Let me tell you about it.

One day, I felt a powerful urge to go fly-fishing. Honestly, the urge is always there; I will never turn down an opportunity to get outside and wet a line. Even so, this time it was different. It felt like God was inviting me, nudging me, to get outside and spend some time with Him out on the water. In my quiet times, God has been showing me just how healing it can be to connect with Him in outdoor moments.

So, I took a day off. I planned a trip with a friend to a quiet mountain lake to catch some trout and hang out with God. This little lake is my favorite spot to fish. I have spent several glorious days there—days that remind me how good life can be.

I was very much looking forward to some rest, relaxation, and restoration. My heart was jumping with excitement. I couldn't wait to dive into this fantastic form of soul care. A friend of mine half-jokingly calls it "better living through fishing." Although amusing, I am inclined to say it is true.

The weather was perfect, and things were off to a wonderful start. We hit the road with high hopes, visions of trout dancing in my mind. But then my car suddenly stopped working. This happened while I was driving on the interstate. I was on a steep incline, headed into the mountains, and I lost all acceleration. Although I had the pedal to the floor, my car had no power. I began slowing to a stop. All around me, cars were blazing by at over 70 mph. Meanwhile, rapidly losing momentum, I had to make my way to the side of the road—uphill and through interstate traffic. Without power, I weaved my way through the mayhem, and safely made it to the shoulder. Scary, to say the least.

Frazzled, I parked the car, and called for roadside assistance. They promised me a tow truck was on its way. So, with growing impatience, I waited for help to arrive.

It was a nerve-wracking scenario, and I was tense. I was stuck in the hot sun, on the side of the highway, stalled out on a curve in the road. As the cars blazed by, many of them shook my car as they passed. Some of them came close to clipping me. I hoped the tow truck would arrive soon to rescue me from this frenzy and end the threat of a rear-end collision from one of these high-speed missiles.

So, in nail-biting tension, I waited. And I waited. Then I waited some more. I waited for hours. Hours! Finally, a tow truck arrived to take my incapacitated car to the shop for repairs.

Having lost several hours waiting on the side of the highway, my amazing day trip was over before it had even begun. All that planning, preparing, and daydreaming; it was all for naught. My hopes were dashed. There would be no day spent landing trout in a picturesque mountain scene. Instead, I had spent a few hours battling frustration, anger, discouragement, disappointment, and fear.

As if all that wasn't bad enough, the enemy took the

opportunity to kick me when I was down. Negative thoughts ran through my mind like a freight train:

"Here you are again. This stuff always happens to you."
"You're never going to be able to have a good trip. Something always happens."
"You're cursed. You can't even get to enjoy a day of fishing with a friend without something going wrong."
"God doesn't care about your day. If He did, He would help."
"See, God doesn't really take care of you. You are always on your own when bad things happen. You have got to figure this out on your own."
"This is terrible. The repair bill will be outrageous. You can't afford for this to happen."
"You will never get ahead in life. Every time you get ahead, something like this always happens."
"Nothing will ever work out for you. Why do you even try?"
"See, God doesn't want good things for you."

The situation was frustrating enough on its own, but when the negative mental dialogue started, it became a miserable experience.

Now, in the grand scheme of things, having my car break down and losing a day of leisure isn't a tragic thing. One challenging day is hardly a blip on the timeline of any of our lives. No doubt, we have all experienced worse things. The overall impact on my life was miniscule.

However, the impact this day had on my heart, well that is a different story.

Heart Attacks

Our hearts are sensitive. They are vulnerable in ways that astound us, scare us, and unnerve us. Our hearts are tender in more ways than we like to admit. Life, with its constant challenges, trials, and traumas, can wreak havoc on our hearts.

Satan knows this. Satan exploits this.

The devil does his best work when he uses the troubles and traumas of life to convince us that his lies are true. He waits patiently for the moment when our hearts are most vulnerable. Then he pounces:

"See, God doesn't really love you."

"Can't you see, nobody wants you around."

"You're broken and ugly. Nobody will ever love you."

"You can't trust anybody. If they actually knew you, they would reject you."

"God did this to you. He is the one holding you down."

"You are on your own in life. It's time you face it."

"Why bother? Nothing ever works out for you."

"Who are you kidding? You can't do that."

"Who do you think you are? It's arrogant to think you will ever find anything better than this."

"It's hopeless. Why don't you just give up? Things will never change."

This is how our enemy operates. He whispers lies into our thoughts, into our hearts. His words are toxic—poison meant to put us down, steal our hope, blame God, and leave us feeling defeated. Much like an abusive narcissist, he spews disparaging remarks meant to discourage us and hold us back.

Like a predator, Satan often attacks when we are most vulnerable. Scripture compares him to a lion (1 Pet. 5:8). He prowls around looking for an opportunity to pounce on the weak, weary, and wounded.

As I sat beside the road that day, battling with my frustration and disappointment, I made an easy target. While I smoldered with sullen indignation, the enemy's lies came like flaming arrows aimed right at my heart.

Some of you might ask, *"Why would the devil care? Why would it matter to him whether or not you go fishing?"*

Well, to be honest, I don't know if the devil does care about fishing or car troubles. Maybe the only reason that Satan cared is because all this mattered to me.

It truly mattered to me. Therefore, it mattered to the enemy.

Your Heart Matters

But it didn't matter just to the enemy. Let me go out on a limb and suggest to you that it mattered to God too.

God cares about the things that matter to me, and He cares about the things that matter to you.

God designed me in such a way that I love fly-fishing. It does something for me that is hard to explain. It grounds me, refreshes me. It nourishes my soul. Angling is like a living, breathing version of Psalm 23, "he leads me beside peaceful streams. He renews my strength" (Ps. 23:3 NLT). When I spend time out on the water, I experience God leading me deeper into His peace. He restores my soul.

Over the years, God has nudged me, urged me, and even commanded me to go fishing. He has given me some amazing opportunities to go on some outstanding fishing trips. He has even inspired me with dreams to combine my love of fly-fishing with ministry. I often daydream about how powerful it could be to provide spiritual direction to other men while we spend some time out on the water.

Fishing matters to me, and because of that, it matters to God.

In case you doubt that God cares about fishing, let me remind you that Jesus gave Peter a miraculous fishing experience on at least three occasions (Luke 5:1-11, Matt. 17:24-27, John 21:1-8).

God cares about the things that matter to us. He cares

about the desires of our hearts. He cares about them because He loves us. He cares about them because He gave them to us. He designed each of us with a unique soul, an inner being like no other. He made us to care about the things we love.

He designed you with your own particular idiosyncrasies. He made you to love fishing, or dancing, or art, or sports, or birdwatching, or basket-weaving, or whatever unique thing you love. You care about these things because God made you that way. He cares about you, and, therefore, cares about the things that matter to you.

Because the desires of your heart matter to God, He wants to share in those experiences with you. Jesus stands at the door and knocks. He wants you to invite Him in and allow Him to join you in the things you love.

Every single thing that matters to you has the potential to become a place where you can experience a deeper connection with God. True fellowship with God begins with sharing meaningful moments with Him.

What is it that matters to you? Losing weight? Getting your business off the ground? Raising your kids? Having a baby? Healing an illness? Landing that new job? Getting out of an unpleasant situation? Whatever it is, I guarantee you it matters to God. Your heart's desires are important to Him.

Now, I am not promising that you will always get what you want or that every desire you have will be satisfied. As I am sure you know, life doesn't work that way. Some of our desires will have to wait until heaven before they are fully satisfied. Still, I want you to know that the things that matter most to your heart also matter to God. His heart cares about your heart.

Our desires create prime opportunities for us to encounter God. Yet, they are also prime opportunities for the enemy to rob and wound us. Because your heart is important—and because God cares about you—the enemy will attack you. Those precious places within your heart are the same places where you will face the enemy's greatest assaults. Satan is strategic. He will attack you in the places that matter most.

The devil will launch his fiercest campaigns against your heart.

Whispered Warfare

God has a plan, purpose, and destiny in mind for you. He made you for eternal joy. He made you to make a powerful impact on the world around you.

The devil also has plans for you.

Whereas God loves you and has a good plan for your life, Satan hates you and has a plan to destroy you. He wants to lay waste to everything God loves, including you. The devil is passionate about robbing you. He is out to "steal and kill and destroy" every good thing in your life (John 10:10).

Yet, for all his malice, our enemy has limited power. He can't simply annihilate any of us or he would have done so by now. You might remember that Satan had to ask God's permission before he could afflict Job or come against Peter (Job 1:9-12, 2:4-6; Luke 22:31).

Satan wages a fierce war against the people of God, but his ability to directly assault us is limited. He seldom launches frontal assaults and direct confrontations, so the devil opts for a more subversive strategy; he lies.

Deception is the defining characteristic of our enemy's personality. He is the "father of lies" (John 8:44). Spreading false narratives and lying accusations are the devil's greatest weapons. He is a master of his craft. He has, after all, had a long time to practice.

Since the beginning of history, Satan has twisted the facts. He aims to spin a different version of the truth, to get us to believe a different story than the one God is telling. In some form or another, we have all fallen for one of his lies. Scripture says that the devil has deceived the whole world (Rev. 12:9).

Our enemy is spreading lies. Through a campaign of deception, the devil whispers toxic stories that twist the facts. Satan's narratives offer a false interpretation of our lives. He designs his lies to lead us away from God, and into blindly following a false path. If we listen to his lies, it will shape how we see God, ourselves, and life itself.

These attacks on our hearts and minds, these assaults on the stories we believe, are the essence of spiritual warfare.

The devil does his best work from the shadows, and most spiritual attacks aren't overt demonic manifestations. Demons seldom lunge out of the shadows or throw furniture around the room. While things like that may occasionally happen, the vast majority of spiritual attacks are more subtle. Our enemy is insidious.

Most spiritual attacks come as thoughts whispered to us, and the most damaging battles happen within our own hearts and minds. Authors Sarah Thiessen and Heather Hughes describe it this way: "It starts out as a little whisper in our ear. Then that whisper takes root and we begin to embrace it. Once we buy into the lie, it becomes our reality."[1]

Demonic forces get their hooks into us when we begin to believe their lies. The thoughts may seem benign at first, but given time to take root and develop, they actually have the power to kill. Like tiny weeds that sprout and eventually lead to an infestation, the devil's lies are designed to go viral. His aim is to subtly guide our thinking toward the very things that will rob us of our joy and destroy our destinies.

When the devil whispers his lies to us, he does it with such precision that we often mistake his ideas for our own. His demonic ideas work well when they are camouflaged inside our own inner dialogue. His whispers are meant to blend in with our thoughts. These attacks come at us with such sly subtly that we seldom suspect that we are actually under attack.

Satan spins a deceptive narrative in order to influence our

thinking for the worse. He wants us to misinterpret the events of our lives, so we fall victim to his strategies. His aim is to convince us to live a different plan than the one God has destined for us.

Spiritual warfare is primarily a matter of believing the right story.

If we don't recognize the warfare for what it is and stand against it, we will unwittingly agree with the lies of our enemy. That means the most basic aspect of spiritual warfare is to recognize lies and stand with the truth.

Joining sides with the true story is the most powerful spiritual thing we can do.

War Stories

Stories are powerful. Stories help us make sense out of life.

Our lives are full of narratives—both good and bad—that help us understand who we are, and our place in the world. The stories we tell ourselves determine how we see ourselves. They help us develop a framework for how we fit into the larger story of history.

Without narratives to explain our experiences, life would feel hazardous and chaotic. Without the framework of a story to underpin our experiences, life would seem like an endless sequence of meaningless events. Stories help us understand and interpret everything we think, feel, and experience.

This may make it seem like narratives are a complicated thing, but stories are simply a way to interpret a series of events. When two people witness the same event—say, for instance, a car crash or robbery—each person remembers the experience somewhat differently. Even though they both witnessed the same event, they will come away from the experience with a story unique to them. They will remember the story, not merely the facts of the situation.

Truth may be a static thing, but people can manipulate

information. We have all heard how you can make statistics say anything you want. Facts can be interpreted and spun in a way that changes the story. In these cases, it isn't so much the facts that matter; rather, it is the narrative that makes all the difference. The situation is like when a biased news reporter spins the facts to fit their own agenda.

God and the devil are both interpreting the events that happen in the world, and in our lives. They see the same events, yet, they are telling different stories.

God wants you to see the things that happen in your life through eyes of faith. God wants you to believe in Him, and trust that He is working for your good.

Satan, on the other hand, tries to get you to interpret the events of your life through a tainted lens. He spins a story that will leave you feeling hopeless, abandoned, and angry at God.

It is crucial we understand the story we are in. Are we living from a narrative that tells that God is with us, that we are forgiven and free? Or are we living out a story that leaves us feeling broken, tired, and fearful?

The stories we believe about God, ourselves, and the people around us will determine how we live our lives. Every single facet of our lives hinges upon the narratives we believe. Every relationship, every interaction we have with others, the work that we do, how we spend our free time, it is all influenced by how we see our own story.

With competing versions of the story vying for our belief, spiritual warfare comes down to this question: *"Whose story do we want to believe?"*

Sharing Our Stories

The best-selling Christian author, John Eldredge, is very familiar with spiritual warfare. He wrote:

The story of your life is the story of the long and brutal assault on your heart by the one who knows what you could be and fears it. I hope you are beginning to see that more clearly now. Otherwise, much of the Bible will not make sense to you. Much of your life will not make sense to you.[2]

It's true, we often don't fully understand our own stories. The majority of time we are too close to see with true clarity. The day-to-day struggles of life and our unresolved pain prevent us from seeing the bigger picture. We develop a kind of spiritual myopia. This near-sightedness keeps us from recognizing how our enemy has wounded and robbed us. Years and years go by without us even recognizing the true source of our trouble.

Jesus said, "the truth will set you free" (John 8:32). Truth sets us free from the lies of the enemy. Knowing the actual story of our lives sets us free from the onslaught of the devil's narrative.

We often discover our own story in the testimony of others. When people candidly share their own victories and struggles, it can help us find new freedom and encouragement.

People in recovery from addictions have a saying. They share their "experience, strength, and hope with each other" when they tell their stories.[3] No sermons. No lectures. No insipid sales pitches. Just open, vulnerable sharing of the ups and downs of what it is like to recover and regain your life from the pit of hell.

In sharing their stories with each other, recovering people help solve their common problem and overcome the damage their addiction has done. In this book, I share stories with you for the same reason. In sharing experience, strength, and hope from the frontlines of spiritual warfare, I want to shed some light on our common problem and help us all recover what we have lost.

I want you to live free, to live from the true story of your life. Spiritual warfare is already affecting you, and those you love. The enemy has robbed every one of us of the joy, purpose, and passion that God dreams for us. The only way we will ever stop this theft is by opening our eyes to the warfare. To do that, we need to share with each other the wisdom we have learned from the trenches.

It is time to recover what we have lost.

It is time to uncover the truth.

It is time to reclaim your story.

TWO

Orphaned Hearts & the Original Lie

The root of all evil is the suspicion that God is not good.

Oswald Chambers

The serpent was the shrewdest of all the wild animals the Lord God had made. One day he asked the woman, "Did God really say you must not eat the fruit from any of the trees in the garden?"

Genesis 3:1 NLT

ALLOW ME TO TELL YOU A LITTLE OF MY OWN STORY.

First of all, you should know my childhood was rough. Where I grew up, alcoholism, addiction, abuse, and shame ran rampant. It was in my family, in my home, in my neighborhood. Every child I knew lived in a broken home. Every adult I knew lived with a broken spirit.

Violence was all around me. At school, at home, even walking down the street. It seemed to follow me wherever I went. So, I learned how to take a punch early on. It was a necessary life skill growing up.

Later, after I got a little older and escaped the violence, I needed to have sinus surgery to take care of an infection. After the surgery, in which the doctor had rearranged my nasal structure, he looked at me with a mixture of concern and awe. Impressed and perplexed, he made a statement which was really more of a question: *"It looks like you've had your nose broken somewhere between seven and eleven times?"*

I was surprised that he could see something like that. I didn't know how to respond. All I could say was, *"Yeah, that sounds about right."* Yet, I still wondered if he estimated a little low.

Even with all the nose breaks, my back took most of the beatings. There were many times my "caretakers" pounded on me. They beat me with closed fists while they called me foul names—the kinds of things I wouldn't dare to repeat in good company.

I learned to cover my head and check out. I went to another place in my mind while I waited for their rage to subside. I reached a point where I could no longer feel the pain. My mind would go blank, and my soul would grow numb. Psychologists call it dissociation. It is the mind's amazing ability to disconnect from something that is too painful to process in the present moment.

While I learned to tune out the physical pain, the verbal attacks caused a trauma that I couldn't escape. Kids have a saying, *"sticks and stones may break my bones, but names will never hurt me."* Sometimes I would whisper this to myself—always under my breath for fear they would hear me—but even back then I knew the little poem was a lie. Harsh words and violent attacks on my identity sunk deep into my soul. There they twisted my insides and shaped my heart into something I eventually grew to hate.

As I got older, I made my way in and out of foster care. Then, in and out of institutions. I never knew where my next "home" might be. It is a strange thing to move from place to place, from house to house. People always surrounded me, yet I never felt so alone.

My formative years were a tumultuous time filled with confusion, heartache, abandonment, pain, and violence. Looking back, I can see the devil's fingerprints all over my childhood. Back then, it was my normal. It was the only life I had ever known.

Everyone bears responsibility for their own choices in life —including those who failed me as a child. Yet, I know that behind every foul word, behind every act of violence, the enemy was right there, egging it all on. Encouraging all the evil.

The devil's noxious narratives were there my entire life. I heard these messages over and over again. They became ingrained in me. They defined everything I did.

"You're weak. Stupid. Lazy."
"Nobody wants you."
"You're a worthless disappointment."
"Something is wrong with you. You're broken. Defective."
"Everybody gave up on you a long time ago. You are a lost cause."
"You'll die alone."
"Nobody would care if you died tonight."

Sometimes people said these things to me. Sometimes I said them to myself. Every time the enemy was there, ready to inspire another round of toxic thoughts.

I heard, *"You'll wind up in jail and die in prison before you turn eighteen,"* so many times I believed it. Everyone said it. Everyone believed it. It seemed like truth to me too, so I lived like it was my story. I drank, stole, and fought like it was my destiny to live and die that way.

Like so many others who grew up in dysfunction, I repeated

the same cycle. I looked around at the brokenness in the lives around me and I felt consigned to the same fate. Their lives taught me not to hope. In turn, my own life experience taught me that I was destined for pain. I thought I was doomed to be a punching bag for life. So, I acted like a broken soul, living with a death-wish.

I aimed to snatch as much as I could from life before I met my end. I lived in pursuit of only the things that made me feel good. This was the only path that made sense to me because I never believed I was going anywhere. I never believed that I mattered, never believed that I had anything better to hope for. I had given myself over to a hopeless story. I fully expected to die before I ever reached adulthood. Because of that, I drank to blot it all out.

Before I was halfway through my teens, I was already addicted to alcohol. I was also experienced in other harder things. I dropped out of high school. I chose a criminal life-style over education. I slept all day and ran around all night. I lived in a perpetual blur; one long blackout punctuated by brief moments of lucidity. Most of the time I woke up without knowing where I was or how I got there. Life was chaotic, exciting, dangerous, and… miserable.

Most of what happened next is a story for another day. However, let me fast forward and tell you that, thanks to the grace of God, that wasn't the end of my story.

Not only did I survive my younger teenage years, I finally came to a place where I was ready to meet my Maker. When I came to know Christ in my early twenties, I had made a colossal mess of my life. Desperation drove me to Him, although I doubted He existed. I was an angry agnostic. Though I hated the idea of God, I still sought after Him. I was out of options, and I knew it.

During my last days as an unbeliever, things went from bad to worse. I was trying to get my life on track—daring to live out a better story. I had already quit drinking (and every-thing else too) a few years prior. I was working hard to clean up the wreckage of my life. I had made great progress, but I was still living in a shaky state. It felt like a house of cards, where one wrong move and my whole life would collapse.

Ruthless as he is, the enemy took advantage of my vulnerable condition and pounced. Evil hit me hard. The spiritual attacks became overt, and overwhelming. The forces of darkness assailed me constantly. Nightmares kept me from sleeping. During the day, I saw apocalyptic visions of people being consumed by hellfire. I had the constant feeling that I was being watched, and I often saw demonic shadow figures move in and out of my periphery. Fearful of being attacked, my eyes would constantly dart from one shadow to the next.

Sometimes the shadowy figures would disappear when I turned to face them. Other times, they didn't. I still get chills when I remember staring into the cold, black eyes of those dark silhouettes.

I lived in a state of perpetual anxiety. It bordered on panic. I felt like I was losing my mind. Dark thoughts ran through my head like a screaming freight train. I longed to drown them out, to return to the oblivion of the bottle.

A tiny flicker of hope, or maybe faith, was the only thing that stood between me and a drink. Looking back, I see the miracle of it—God saving me from myself. Back then, I couldn't see it. All I could see was the pain I was going through.

Desperate and pleading, I would often cry to God to make it all stop. Yet, whenever I would pray, foul "voices" intruded upon my thoughts. They bombarded me with their criticisms: *"Unwanted. Broken. Dirty. Shameful. Worthless. Hopeless."* On and on they would berate me.

The demonic voices mocked me relentlessly. Full of derision and scorn, they would laugh at me saying, *"God has abandoned you."* They warned me never to go to church. They said that church folk were too wholesome to tolerate *"a piece of human excrement"* like me. The demonic voices constantly threatened me with damnation. I crumpled under their constant barrage. I believed their condemning lies. I could almost feel the heat of hell's flames coming for me. Once again, I felt like my story was over.

The day that I gave my life to Jesus, I was beyond desperate. Anything had to be better than the hell I was living in. I hit my knees and said a simple prayer, *"I'm in."* With that humble beginning, everything changed.

Immediately, I saw an incredible vision. In my mind's eye, I saw into the unseen realm. All around me the invisible assailants became visible. The shadows became clear. I could now see every dark and cruel voice as the foul evil that it was. Dozens, hundreds, perhaps thousands of demons surrounded me. They pressed in on me, threatening to crush me under the sheer weight of their dark presence.

I saw myself from a view outside of myself. I watched as I kneeled and said my prayer to Jesus. Then, just as all hope seemed lost, I saw a black hole open directly above me. Like a vacuum, the vortex pulled every demon out of my room and into an abyss. Within an instant, it sucked every bit of darkness from the room.

One moment I was on the verge of destruction. Then, in the blink of an eye, the whole situation was different. I was now alone in the room. Sunlight poured through the windows, and my mind was quieter than it had ever been.

Life, Death, and Lies

Most people don't experience spiritual warfare as intensely as I did back then (although, over the years, I have talked with many people who can relate to my story all too well). Most of the time, spiritual warfare isn't nearly as overt. Our enemies—the spiritual forces of evil (Eph. 6:12)—prefer to avoid obvious attacks. Whether we are talking about the devil himself or his demonic horde of evil spirits, their tactics are the same. Evil prefers to operate from the shadows. Its agents love to attack in sneakier, subtler ways.

Usually the spiritual warfare we face comes from the temptation to believe Satan's false narratives. He assaults us with a battery of lies, misinterpretations, untrue stories, false narratives, ungodly ideas, limiting beliefs, and cognitive distortions.

Spiritual warfare is a battle of propaganda.

The devil peddles perverted versions of the truth to trip us up, hold us back, and hold us down. When we believe his lies and act upon those faulty beliefs, we become accomplices in our own demise. Every temptation to sin begins with the temptation to believe the devil's lies.

Truth is our biggest weapon in this conflict. Knowing and applying the truth is both an offensive and a defensive strategy in spiritual warfare. Why? Because the stories we believe make all the difference. Our lives conform to the narratives we embrace. We always live out the stories we believe.

Scripture says, "life and death are in the power of the tongue" (Prov. 18:21). The words that we say have immense power to shape how we live. This is also true for the things we think. Life and death truly are in the power of our thoughts.

The story I grew up believing defined my early life. I thought I was hopeless, worthless, a punching bag for life. Those narratives gave the devil power in my life. They were the narratives of death. Believing those stories almost killed me.

What kinds of lies has your heart been told?

What stories have you believed?

Believing the right narrative can literally be a matter of life and death. In fact, death entered all of our stories because of one of Satan's lies.

A Snake in Paradise

The devil is the master deceiver; the first and foremost liar. Jesus called him "the father of lies" (John 8:44). The original sin, and humanity's subsequent fall, happened when our first parents fell prey to one of the devil's schemes.

I am sure you remember the story. Free and unashamed, Adam and Eve were blissfully spending their days in paradise. Everything was perfect. All was well and life was "very good" (Gen. 1:31).

Then evil entered the scene.

Scripture gives our enemy many names: Satan (Job 1:6), the devil (Matt. 4:1), the tempter (Matt. 4:3), the accuser (Rev. 12:10), the evil one (Matt. 13:19), the father of lies (John 8:44), and the dragon (Rev. 12:9). The Bible also calls him the serpent (Gen. 3:1, Rev. 12:9). This is an especially fitting name for our enemy, who twists the truth within his conniving coils. Unbelievably crafty, he knows how to distort the facts, get inside our heads, and lead us astray.

A few years ago, my wife and I came across an exceptional children's Bible, *The Jesus Storybook Bible*. We often read it to our kids. It brings the biblical stories to life in a way that a child's heart can easily understand. The way it paints the picture in Genesis chapter 3 is especially helpful to our conversation.

As soon as the snake saw his chance, he slithered silently up to Eve. "Does God really love you?" the serpent whispered. "If he does, why won't he let you eat the nice, juicy, delicious fruit? Poor you, perhaps God doesn't want you to be happy."

The snake's words hissed into her ears and sunk down deep into her heart, like poison. *Does God love me?* Eve wondered. Suddenly she didn't know anymore.

"Just trust me," the serpent whispered. "You don't need

God. One small taste, that's all, and you'll be happier that you could ever dream…"[1]

You know the rest of the story. The serpent deceived Eve. She, and Adam, listened to the enemy's venomous story. The consequences were dire. Paradise was lost. Death entered the human story, and with it came sickness, selfishness, toil, and pain.

> And a terrible lie came into the world. It would never leave. It would live on in every human heart, whispering to every one of God's children: "God doesn't love me."[2]

The serpent's lies live on in each one of our lives. The doubts he cast upon the goodness of God and the aspersions he made on God's character continue to plague all humanity.

Orphaned Hearts

The Fall brought confusion and doubt into our relationship with God. It continues to make us all struggle to believe in God's goodness and to trust His heart toward us. Every human heart has felt the pain of separation. Every one of us knows loss.

Yet, this isn't what God wants for us. Death wasn't a part of God's original design for humanity. Neither was grief, pain, or sadness. One day, God will finally free us from these hurtful hardships. In that glorious day, "there will be no more death or sorrow or crying or pain" (Rev. 21:4 NLT). All of those things will cease forever because they were never what God wanted for His children.

God wants good things for His people. He gives good things to us (James 1:17). He has good plans in mind for us (Jer. 29:11). In the beginning, everything He created was only good, or very good (Gen. 1:31). He created people to live freely in that delightful paradise.

Even though times have changed, and we no longer live in the Garden of Eden, God's desire for humanity hasn't changed. He will restore everything (Acts 3:21). God will bring us back to the goodness of the garden. He wants us to live forever in happiness and joy. He wants good things for us. As Scripture says, every good and perfect thing in life is a gift from Him (James 1:17).

This means God wants good things for you. God wants you to have a good life.

It is important that we know this—that we really grasp this truth deep down in our bones. It is important that we know this because life in our fallen world will test us. It will challenge our belief that God is good, that He loves us, and that He desires to give us good things.

The origin of all evil lies in the suspicion that God isn't good. The attack in the Garden of Eden was an attack on the character of God. The enemy tricked Adam and Eve into believing that God wasn't good, that they couldn't trust him, and that it would be better if they took matters into their own hands.

From the beginning, Satan has been casting aspersions on God's character. He peddles a narrative that says that we can't trust the heart of our God. The lies he spreads say that we are on our own, like spiritual orphans.

Humanity took the bait. We lost a perfect connection with our Heavenly Father. Now we all struggle to fend off the enemy's lies. Our hearts wonder if we can trust God. We wonder if He will come through for us. We doubt that He truly will. We suspect that we are really on our own. We suffer the pain of a heart that feels orphaned by God.

Think about it for a moment. Where in your life do you struggle to trust God?

Even when we know in our minds that God has good

things waiting for us, it can still be a struggle to bring our hearts into agreement. Our hearts are wounded; they have trust issues. Our hearts harbor secret fears, crushing disappointments, and deep-rooted pain.

Those wounds compound and make us even more vulnerable to the enemy's lies. Like Adam and Eve, we too can fall prey to the stories that can lead us astray.

Hooks and Snares

The devil is very good at what he does. His lies are hard to spot. Often, they seem perfectly reasonable; deception presented as something believable.

The lies seem true because they usually contain elements of truth. All good lies do. A good lie is believable because it takes parts of the truth and twists them just enough to make the deception seem plausible.

In his book, *When the Enemy Strikes*, Charles Stanley explains that, "The lies of the devil always have a ring of truth to them. The best counterfeit is always as close to the authentic item as possible. The same for the best lie—it's just one degree from the truth."[3]

As I said, I love to fly-fish. However, I must confess a secret about being an angler: being a fisherman is basically being a liar.

All anglers are liars. Every last one of them.

Now, I don't mean that we are liars because we like to tell exaggerated fish stories (although that is often the case). What I mean is that the very act of fishing is a lie. Fishing is simply practicing the art of deception with some fancy gear.

Fish may not be the smartest creatures in the food chain, but they aren't dumb enough to swallow something that looks harmful. When you are trying to catch a fish, you present it with something that appears real, something that seems tasty and desirable. A big, shiny, exposed fishhook won't do it. You must hide the hook and deceive the fish, in order to catch it.

Thus, we anglers go to great lengths to deceive fish. We either bait the hooks with something tasty or we disguise the hooks themselves. We hide the hooks—things that can only bring pain or death to the fish—inside something that looks healthy, nourishing, and desirable to the unsuspecting creature.

Likewise, the devil's lies come carefully camouflaged inside enough truth to make them palatable. The lies have to seem like the truth. When lies are blatantly obvious, no one takes the bait. Thus, Satan presents his stories in ways that seem believable. Skillfully, he interprets the events of our lives in a convincing way. When we believe his lies—take the bait and agree with the devil's narrative—he gets his hooks into us.

Every time we believe one of Satan's stories, he establishes a foothold in our minds. It gives evil a beachhead, a point of access to our lives. To say it simply, deception gives the demonic realm power over us.

Each lie we believe opens the door wider until the lies become embedded into our thinking. The enemy gains more influence in our thought life and continues to spew even more falsehoods. The more the cycle progresses, the more power the enemy has over us. Soon, lies define our reality, and darkness has all the power it needs to sabotage our lives.

The Attacks Start Early

Satan doesn't fight fair.

Though his tactics may be subtle, his intentions are heartless and cruel. Not only does our enemy love to kick us when we are down, the devil loves to prey on those who are innocent and most vulnerable.

The enemy specifically targets children.

Satan targets children for two reasons. One, children are

precious to God. Our God is a good Father—the best one. Like any good father, He loves His kids. His heart yearns for their good and He wants to see them do well in life. In fact, Jesus tells us we should become more childlike; that life in the kingdom of God depends on it (Matt. 18:3).

Our Lord loves us all, but He has a special place in His heart for kids. Satan, on the other hand, hates us all. He also hates God, and therefore the devil "especially hates what God loves most, our children."[4] Our enemy hates children; he seeks to destroy the Lord's cherished ones.

In his insightful work, *The Handbook for Spiritual Warfare*, Dr. Ed Murphy says that the second reason that Satan targets children is because it is "the most strategic way to destroy humanity."[5] Evil knows that if it can inflict enough damage on a child, then it can derail that youngster's entire life.

A few targeted attacks on a young life can sabotage that person and cause a lifetime of suffering. The wounds we experience in our formative years have a tendency to stick with us throughout our lifetime. Sometimes we spend the rest of our lives in reaction to the toxic narratives we took on in childhood.

When we are young, we have little choice except to go with the flow and accept what comes our way. We try to make sense of the world as best we can. Yet, as children, we don't have the experience or wisdom we need to look at life critically and objectively.

So, when painful experiences happen, we rarely realize there might be more than one way to interpret them. If no one is there to guide us to the truth, to help interpret life for us, Satan is more than happy to do so.

Yet, even in the best of childhoods, we all still suffer emotional wounds. In this fallen world, there seems to be no way to make it through childhood without collecting a few inner scars.

A Tragic Misinterpretation

The enemy's lies don't have to be big in order to have a big impact. Often, simple misunderstandings can provide all the enemy needs to derail our lives.

A few years ago, Susie shared a story of how Jesus set her free from the burden of feeling unwanted. She struggled her entire life to feel adequate, wanted, and loved. She doubted that anyone ever really wanted her around. This kept her socially isolated and prevented her from truly enjoying relationships. Well into middle age, such inner beliefs affected every relationship, even with her husband and children.

God set Susie free of this burden through a specialized ministry session. During the session, she asked Jesus to take her back to the root of the issue. Her mind immediately went back to a scene from her childhood. She recalled an incident that happened when she was three years old.

It was a family gathering. Many relatives filled her house and gathered together in the kitchen. After a bit of time playing with the other children, she set off to say hello to the grown-ups. With a child's excitement, she entered the kitchen. She expected them to greet her with as much excitement as she had for them. Yet, instead of welcoming her, they suddenly became silent. They were visibly uncomfortable and seemed impatient to have her leave.

The moment hit her hard. She felt devastated and unwanted. Though no one realized, this simple moment was a turning point in her life.

The devil took advantage of the event. He whispered to her young heart, "*See, nobody wants you around.*"

Just a child. How could she possibly know to counter that kind of deception? She believed the lie.

The toxic idea took root. In time it spread. It set in motion a new lens with which she interpreted the world. From then on, every time Susie experienced some form of rejection, it confirmed the lie. Over and over, life gave her plenty of reason to reinforce the lie, for her to claim it as truth.

By the time Susie reached mid-life, it held her captive. The deeply rooted conviction that she was unwanted and unlovable held her heart in bondage. It astounds me that a lifetime of feeling unwanted had its origin in such a commonplace event that happened to her at such a young age. Over fifty years of loneliness were born in a moment of agreement with a lying narrative.

Thankfully, she found freedom. In her ministry session, she asked God to speak truth into her pain. She asked Jesus to expose the lie and reveal the truth.

In an amazing experience, God reinterpreted her story. Together, she and Jesus walked through her memory of that pivotal event. As they retraced the steps, He showed her how this momentous day was meant to be special for a different reason. He reminded her it was the day before her birthday, the day before her family threw her a great big party.

That one detail reframed the entire story. Suddenly, the scene took on a new meaning. Through the eyes of an adult, she saw it all differently. She saw that her family had gathered in the kitchen to make preparations for the celebration. When she came in the room, it caught them off guard. They awkwardly ushered her out of the room so she wouldn't overhear their plans.

Her heart suddenly had a new interpretation to the story. The realization hit her—she wasn't unwanted. In fact, many people had come together just to celebrate her special day. She was deeply loved, and all of her family had gathered to make her feel special!

That truth changed everything for her. From that point on, she no longer viewed her life through the lens of an unwanted child. Deep within, she knew she was loved. The truth transformed her experience in the present.

When she let go of the toxic narrative that she was

unwanted, the entire story unraveled. The lie lost its grip on her life. Without that stranglehold, rejection no longer threatened with its painful sting. It could no longer hurt her heart like it had in the past. Half a century of bondage no longer defined her story.

Everything changed from that point forward.

Trauma and Wounding

With the previous story, you can see how one little lie had a profoundly damaging effect on the woman. It proves that the wounds we experience don't have to be traumatic to have a crippling effect on our lives.

Yet, when we experience trauma, the result can be devastating.

Accidents, abuse, abandonment, death, and loss cut deep and leave lasting scars. Although we humans are a resilient lot, capable of surviving extreme things, these experiences leave a mark. Such inner wounds, the scars on our hearts, continue to ache long after the original pain has passed.

Often the stories we believe because of that pain do us more harm than the original wounding.

I have counseled many people—both men and women— who suffered abuse as children. For some, the abuse was physical. For others, it was sexual. For many, it was both.

The impact on their lives is impossible to quantify. Years after the original abuse, the aftereffects still linger; they bleed into nearly every area of life. Often these people have trouble relaxing. They seldom fully let down their guard or truly rest in the presence of another. These individuals often suffer with other issues, such as anger, anxiety, and addiction. Many have trouble forming healthy relationships and struggle to find appropriate intimacy.

While the original abuse was terrible and traumatic, the ongoing damage comes from the narratives these people came to believe because of the abuse. Damaging, demonic thoughts continue to haunt them for decades:

"You're dirty."
"There is something wrong with you."
"You can't trust anyone. You will never be safe."
"You can't get close to anybody. They will hurt you too."
"Nobody wants you. No one will ever love you."
"Nobody good will ever want to be with you. You're damaged goods."
"It was your fault. You deserved it."
"You should be ashamed of yourself."
"You are only good for sex."

Trauma survivors hear foul messages like these (they come in a million forms) all the time. Sometimes the broken narratives continue for the rest of their lives. They hear these kinds of demonic lies so often, for so long, that they just assume they are the truth. The lies become a part of their reality. They replay over and over. Silently running in the background, they subtly affect how these individuals see the world. Once the lies take root, they spread until they infect every part of a person's life. Unless these lies are confronted and countered with truth, they spoil everything worthwhile in life.

Victims twice, these survivors not only suffer the initial violation, they live with the damaging effects of a demonic inner dialogue that hounds them relentlessly. The enemy's damning narratives sabotage their friendships, relationships, health, happiness, and hopes. The devil's deceptions drag hurting souls down into the miry depths of despair. Convinced that the dark narratives are true, these poor souls lose all hope for a better future.

Given enough time, the devil's deceit will drive a wedge between the victim and the rest of the world; the lies ruin any chance at true intimacy with another person, or with God.

Torn in Two

Jenny was a bright, young Christian woman who came to counseling with a serious problem. She felt hopelessly stuck in an emotionally abusive relationship.

She described her boyfriend as a narcissist with a dark personality. He was brooding, temperamental, and self-absorbed. Interested in Satanism, he dabbled in the dark arts.

Jenny felt drawn to him like a moth to a flame. She felt compelled to pursue him. Though she often hated him, she was obsessed with him.

Their relationship was emotionally volatile and was progressing toward physical violence. There was a complete absence of any kind of loving communication. True intimacy was a joke. Her boyfriend put her down all the time. He knew how to make his words cut deep. With surgical precision, he would attack her weakest points, ensuring she would stay small.

Things kept getting worse. Red flags waved all over the place. She called their relationship a living hell. She wanted out. Yet, she stayed with him.

Her friends urged her to get out. She would follow their advice and break up with him, but then she would go back. She would hide this from her friends because she didn't want them to know.

The cycle repeated over and over. She would leave, make a new start. Then she would get lonely and eventually go back to him. She kept going back, even though she knew how the story would go.

Jenny came to counseling hoping to break the cycle.

Right away, I could see that the devil's lies and a wounded story were the root of her troubles. Although she was bright and beautiful, she never believed that a good man would want to be with her. She believed that she was too broken, sullied, and stained for anyone good to want her. So, she never considered that she might deserve better than the boyfriend she had. She believed this cycle of abuse was the best she could ever hope for.

This was the devil's intent—to convince her to settle for scraps. Over the years, evil had attacked her with so many damaging words:

"Nobody could ever love you."
"You're disgusting, dirty, broken."
"God doesn't love you. How could he forgive you?"
"Nobody cares how you feel."
"This is the best you will ever get."
"The only thing you have to offer anybody is your body."
"Sex is the only way you will ever get any attention."

The lies had roots in her childhood. Although nobody directly said these exact words, the narratives wormed their way in all the same. Satan got his hooks into Jenny through the dysfunction that surrounded her growing up.

Jenny's parents struggled with issues of their own. As a child, she felt abandoned, sidelined as her parents wrestled with their own demons. Jenny wanted more of their attention. She needed healthy emotional attachment. Yet, she fell between the cracks. Lonely and lost, something isolated her from the attentiveness and affirmation she needed. Even though her family was always close by, she still felt alone.

The evil one took advantage of her pain and bombarded her with his condemning dialogue. Sadly, Jenny's life had a lot of pain, and, even worse, every painful experience, every emotional wound she experienced reinforced the devil's narrative. Whenever someone failed to notice her, he would whisper, *"Nobody cares."* When she got older and boys began to notice her, the enemy was right there murmuring, *"Guys only notice you because they want to have sex with you."* There was no one in her life to counter the lies with God's truth.

The deceptive story felt so true that naturally she believed it. Jenny listened to the foul narratives for so long they became a part of her inner dialogue. She repeated them to herself, agreeing with the lies. Unaware that she had partnered with the enemy's deceit, she now talked to herself in the same damaging way. By the time she met this boyfriend, the devil had firmly established his damaging dialogue in her heart. Trouble was inevitable.

Jenny's entire life felt defined by the weight of her brokenness. It felt like a miserable future was the best she could ever hope for. She hated her prison of a relationship, yet, in her heart, she believed she deserved it.

Wounded, confused, and stuck, Jenny cried out to God. He answered in an amazing way.

She saw a vision. She pictured herself being ripped apart, torn in two. The devil had her by one arm. Jesus was holding onto the other. Like a tug of war, they pulled her in two directions at the same time. Satan was leading her astray, trying to drag her down into the fires of hell. Jesus took her by the hand, trying to lead her into the light of freedom. She felt split down the middle.

Jesus wanted to lead her out of her darkness. Part of her wanted to walk with Him into the light, to listen to His loving words of affirmation. The other part of her heart felt too dirty to go with Jesus. She believed the devil's narrative. Feeling spiritually orphaned, the devil's condemnation felt like truth. It gave the evil one power over her.

The battle was fierce. Trying to follow two masters was literally tearing her apart. It was time for her to make a choice. She could no longer stay in the middle, being torn in two directions. Who would she go with?

While the devil's narrative was familiar, she knew his road would lead her to ruin. That path kept her running in circles, repeating the same mistakes over and over again. Even though she couldn't imagine a better life for herself, she was desperate to find something new. Out of options, she tried something different.

Freedom came when she rejected the devil's narrative and stepped closer to Christ. When she made her approach, she still had lingering doubts and feelings of unworthiness. Yet, she decided to let go of her old identity. It was a miserable life, and she wanted something more. She wanted to believe that God had something better in mind for her. It had to be better. She couldn't imagine things getting any worse.

For her, this was a step of faith. She had to step beyond her feelings, and into uncertain territory. Like Peter, who walked on water (Matt 14:22-33), she had to step out of the boat—out of the realm of the familiar—and into uncharted seas.

She simply chose to trust, though she didn't feel like trusting. Yet, when she made the choice to trust Jesus, everything shifted.

She saw another scene. This time the devil was gone. It was just her and Jesus. Warm and friendly, He stood next to her. Gently taking her hand, He led her forward. He led her back to her childhood home. Together, they entered the old familiar house.

Now an adult, the place looked very different to her than it had when she was a child. The house hadn't aged well at all. It was decrepit, worn down, and stuffy. Not a place fit for her to live in anymore.

Jesus showed her the dilapidated old house, which perfectly symbolized how the life she was familiar with was old, worn out, stuffy, and decrepit—a life story no longer fit for living.

Then Jesus showed her something she had never seen before. It was a book. He sat her down, close to His side, and opened up the book.

It was the story of her life. The story of the life God intended for her. It had everything from the time she was born until she would pass. It was full of love and laughter. It was a story of affirmation, joy, and triumph over sorrow. It was a story of light, purity, and peace. It was a story God was proud to tell because He was proud of her. This was her true story, the one God intended for her before she was ever even born.

The warfare unraveled the moment she listened to this new story. The effects were incredible.

When I last spoke with Jenny, her life was on an entirely different footing. She broke it off with her ex and never went back. She experienced a vibrant new connection with God. She stepped out into new work opportunities. Her relationship with friends and family became deeper than she ever imagined possible. She has even risked dating again—this time with a newfound respect for herself, knowing that she deserves better.

Now she is on an entirely different trajectory. When I asked her to describe her transformation, all she could say was, *"Jesus showed me what He wants for my life. And it's good."* She resolved to never again settle for less than God's best.

God wanted more for her. Being the good God that He is, He destined her for a better story. Now, she is living that story.

A better story awaits you as well. Just like with Jenny, the battle is to believe what Jesus says is true. God has a good plan in mind for you. He wants more for you than you know. In order to live that life, it is necessary that you break any agreements you have made with the devil's lies.

Satan's stories have held you back, and there is no room for his toxic narratives in the amazing future God has planned for you.

THREE

Unholy Agreements & Damaging Inner Dialogues

There is a war going on, and your mind is the battlefield.

Joyce Meyer

The weapons we fight with are not the weapons of the world. On the contrary, they have divine power to demolish strongholds. We demolish arguments and every pretension that sets itself up against the knowledge of God, and we take captive every thought to make it obedient to Christ.

2 Corinthians 10:4-5

My wife and I had just finished an intense ministry session where we helped a woman escape a demonic stronghold that gripped her life. Set free from issues that had influenced her for decades, her newfound freedom was a wonder to behold.

Satan lost some serious ground in her life that night. We reclaimed territory for God's kingdom. It was beautiful to see God begin to write a new story for her. It was definitely a cause for celebration.

You can bet that the enemy was not happy.

Just as I stepped into another room, evil fought back. A hostile voice spoke to me. It came as a dark, bitter thought pressed upon my mind. An unwelcome intrusion into my thoughts by an angry being.

"I will kill you."

Whoa! That grabbed my attention.

I heard it again. *"I am going to kill you."*

Then the repulsive voice added, *"I am coming after you and your family. I will get you. I am going to hurt your kids."*

At first, it startled me. Then I chuckled. I found it amusing. I had heard threats like these before.

Demonic forces are bullies. They like to act tough and threaten you when you are taking ground for God. I have learned to treat these kinds of threats as a sign that I am on the right track. That I am doing something good, something holy—something that darkness hates.

My wife soon joined me. Interestingly, the same thing had just happened to her. A wall of fear hit her, and a vile thought crept into her mind. Another voice. Another threat to our family. The enemy was obviously upset; angry and threatening reprisal.

We smiled.

It was reassuring to know that we had both heard the same thing. It was so encouraging to know that we had struck a blow against Satan's kingdom that night. We took a moment to praise God. Then we commanded the evil to go.

It had no actual power over us. If it had, it would have acted upon it. Instead of threatening us, it would have lashed out to harm us. But it couldn't.

Impotent, its only recourse was to try to intimidate us. It tried to bully us into believing something that wasn't true. This evil spirit wanted us to believe that it had some power to harm us. It didn't.

If we had believed the lie, it would have established a

stronghold of fear. Evil would have terrorized us into submission and made us less likely to minister like this again.

I believe that was the point. The attack was an attempt to scare us out of ministry. It failed.

We didn't buy into the story that the enemy peddled that night. We rejected those toxic thoughts. We chose, instead, to set our thoughts upon the good things we had just witnessed God do.

Our partnership with God as He brought new freedom, and our praise of His faithful goodness, were acts of war. By believing in our God, we took a defiant stance against the lying voice of our enemy.

Hearing Voices

People sure raise an eyebrow when you say you heard a "voice." It does sound a little crazy, right?

I'm sure we have all heard stories of people suffering from mental illness (or severe demonic oppression) who heard a voice that told them to do something awful. Naturally, these kinds of events can make us a little skeptical and uneasy when talking about hearing voices.

Yet, when we set aside the stigma, we can all admit that we hear voices.

Voices run through our minds constantly. Sometimes we hear our thoughts as though they were a voice inside our heads. Our own desires, hurts, and fears parade through our minds, creating an ongoing internal dialogue.

Many of the voices inside our minds come from people who have significantly affected our lives. How often do you hear the voice of your father, mother, or high school gym teacher? Like a mental recording, we remember the things they said. We can still hear their encouragement, or correction, and their influence lives on even after they have gone. I can still hear the voice of my Marine Corps bootcamp drill instructor, Staff Sergeant Cordona, yelling *"Meyers!"*

Sometimes the thoughts we think come from outside of ourselves. It's crucial for Christians to realize that many of the voices we hear inside our minds aren't our own. In fact, many thoughts that we assume are our own actually come from the spiritual realm.

Matthew 16 illustrates how both God and Satan can inspire our thoughts. In one outstanding moment, Peter declares the truth that Jesus is, "the Messiah, the Son of the living God" (Matt. 16:16). Jesus responds, "Blessed are you, Simon son of Jonah, for this was not revealed to you by flesh and blood, but by my Father in heaven" (v. 17).

Jesus tells Peter that this was a revelation. Peter's thoughts came directly from the mouth of God.

Yet, just a few verses later, Peter again feels inspired to say something to Jesus. When Jesus explained that God's plan included his death and resurrection, Peter rebuked Jesus, saying, "This shall never happen to you!" (v. 22).

However, this time Peter had been listening to the wrong voice. Jesus looked at Peter, and said, "Get behind me, Satan! You are a stumbling block to me; you do not have in mind the concerns of God, but merely human concerns" (v. 23). The devil inspired Peter's rebuke of Jesus. In response, Jesus reprimanded Satan, denouncing his deceiving words spoken through the disciple's mouth.

Within the space of a few verses, both God and the devil had imparted a message into Peter's mind. Both heaven and hell had spoken to his thoughts. It is a sobering wake-up call when we realize that the same thing can happen to us.

Not only can it happen, it often does. Referring to the fact that voices can come from a spiritual source, Peter Horrobin observed that, "hearing voices is far more common than most people realize."[1] The voices are usually inaudible; they speak to our hearts and minds, not to our ears. It is rare for anyone to hear an audible voice, whether from God or from the enemy.

God often speaks to us in a "still small voice," just as He did with the prophet Elijah (1 Kings 19:12). Whether He whispers encouragement or correction, His aim is the same: God is always working for our good, speaking words of life into our inner being.

Satan, on the other hand, is out to destroy us. Scripture calls him "the accuser" (Rev. 12:10). He relentlessly lies, condemns, and accuses us of being broken, sullied, and sinful. One of his favorite tricks is to place a sinful thought into our mind and then turn around and tell us what a terrible person we are for thinking such a wicked thing. Satan instigates the issue; he inspires the whole thing, then cruelly shames us.

In his book, *The Bondage Breaker*, Neil Anderson wrote:

> We have all heard his lying, hateful, voice in our hearts and consciences. He never seems to let up on us. Many Christians are perpetually discouraged and defeated because they believe his persistent lies about them. And those who give in to his accusations end up being robbed of the freedom that God intends His people to enjoy.[2]

We have all heard the lying voice of the evil one whispering in our ears. This is how the vast majority of spiritual attacks manifest; they come as thoughts suggested to our minds.

The enemy's lies usually come more quietly than those threats made against me and my family. Evil often prefers to hide its presence. Demonic forces design their foul words to blend in with our own thoughts. Their lies work best when they become camouflaged inside our own inner dialogue.

Scripture says, "Satan, who is the god of this world, has blinded the minds of those who don't believe" (2 Cor. 4:4 NLT). Evil clouds the minds of the world around us. Satan makes it so people can't see clearly. His twisting of truth doesn't just happen to unbelievers—it happens to us all. We Christians also fall prey to the devil's lies. We, too, live in bondage.

So, our fight begins with bringing more truth into our lives. We uproot and expel the lies that hinder us. We can't allow any ungodly, limiting beliefs to occupy space in our minds.

The devil aims to guide our thinking toward the very things that will sabotage our joy and rob us of our destinies. His lies are designed to go viral and spread. Though the thoughts may seem benign at first, if they are allowed to take root, they will eventually destroy our lives.

It is crucial that we learn to recognize and reject the lies. We can't allow the enemy to guide our thoughts with his toxic narrative.

We must fight to reclaim our own headspace.

The Battlefield of the Mind

Let's get one thing abundantly clear: you are not your thoughts.

Your thoughts are part of your life, but they don't define your life. Good, bad, or ugly, your thoughts don't define you.

Not every thought that passes through your mind is even your own. God inspires some thoughts. The enemy inspires others. Though culture has made it a cartoonish caricature, the picture of having an angel on one shoulder and a devil on the other conveys a timeless truth.

Both God and the devil can equally speak thoughts to our minds. This is how spiritual warfare affects every one of us, every single day. The voice of truth clashes with the lies of the enemy, and our mind is the battlefield.

As Christians, our true fight is not with the world or the people in it. Our fight is with dark powers and evil spiritual forces that oppose the goodness of God (Eph. 6:12). Our battles are spiritual battles.

Therefore,

> Though we live in the world, we do not wage war as the world does. The weapons we fight with are not the weapons of the world. On the contrary, they have divine power to demolish strongholds. We demolish arguments and every pretension that sets itself up against the knowledge of God, and we take captive every thought to make it obedient to Christ. (2 Cor. 10:3-6)

We fight spiritual battles by taking our thoughts captive, we reclaim them from Satan. We destroy the strongholds that his toxic narratives have established in our minds.

Anderson expressed it well: "The center of all spiritual bondage is the mind. That's where the battle must be fought and won if you are to experience the freedom in Christ which is your inheritance."[3] Spiritual bondage—enslavement to the enemy—centers in our minds. The thoughts we listen to will determine whether we walk in freedom or defeat.

We take our thoughts captive by recognizing and rejecting lying thoughts. In doing so, we reclaim them by tenaciously steering our thoughts toward truth.

In her book, *The Battlefield of the Mind,* Joyce Meyer explains that, "A stronghold is an area in which we are held in bondage (in prison) due to a certain way of thinking."[4] Once a thought or a certain way of thinking becomes established and habitual, it develops into a mental stronghold. These are the ideas and values that are so deeply rooted we never think to question their validity. They are like mental fortresses; thoughts so entrenched that they distort how we see life.

Often it isn't the circumstances or challenges of life that cause the most trouble. It is our attitudes and ideas that are the real problem. The way we interpret the events of our lives is often more important than the actual events themselves.

A true and right perspective is the key to a free and fulfilling life.

I have seen people transform right before my eyes when they let go of old beliefs that were holding them back. Ungodly, limiting beliefs were the source of their bondage.

We become prisoners to the lies we listen to. We live in bondage to the stories we believe.

Trash Talk

I recently worked with a young man, Eric, who was struggling to overcome a destructive drug habit. He reached out to me after having several relapses in rapid succession.

He wanted to learn coping strategies, some kind of trick to help him turn from temptation the next time it came around. I could see right away that the problem went much deeper than a simple lack of willpower.

I asked, *"Eric, do you like yourself?"*

To my surprise, he answered with an immediate and defensive *"No!"* Suddenly sullen, he had contempt for himself written all over his face.

We spent the next half hour talking about how hatred and disdain for himself were the root of his problem. He hated himself for using drugs. He used drugs because he hated his life. He hated his life because he hated himself. He knew he was stuck, caught in a vicious cycle, spiraling downward.

We examined some of his mindsets, the narratives that were causing him so much trouble. We identified several damaging dialogues running through his mind. Then, we wrote out the lies, and began working to take his thoughts captive to the truth.

One of the key ideas that held him back was the thought, *"You are a piece of garbage."* The actual thought was something far worse, but you get the idea. Eric told me that this condemning thought hounded him nonstop. It harassed him day and night. Anytime he tried to step out and improve his life, it was right there to put him down. When he applied for a job, or tried to meet people, or go to church, or do anything else, there it was again, always tearing him down.

Surprisingly, he could already recognize that this thought came from a voice that sounded different from his own. It was a distinct voice with a cruel hissing tone. He could easily distinguish it from the other thoughts that passed through his mind. Though somewhat skeptical about spiritual warfare, he admitted that he believed that one of the devil's minions was behind this trash talk.

Yet, he still listened to it.

This was the baffling and heartbreaking part of our conversation. He could see how believing this lie was tearing him down. He openly admitted that an evil force was harassing him by spewing this toxic narrative. Even so, he still listened to the lying spirit.

He couldn't, or wouldn't, listen to the idea that the voice might be wrong. He wholeheartedly agreed with it. He wouldn't even consider the possibility that he might not be human trash. Eric remained stubbornly committed to the foul narrative that he was a worthless and no-good piece of garbage. He refused to fight that thought.

He is still in bondage.

Unholy Agreements

In Eric's case, he clearly saw the enemy at work and still listened to the lies. His agreement with the lies gave the enemy permission to influence his life. With that root firmly established, the dark fruit of self-hatred and addiction continues to grow.

Most of the time, we never recognize the enemy is

speaking to us. We assume that the thoughts we think must be our own and, therefore, they must be true. But when we mistake the demonic dialogue for our own thoughts, we inadvertently make an agreement with those lies.

These agreements with the enemy's narrative are the primary way Satan gains power over us. Even when we are unaware, our agreements with evil give demonic spirits the opportunity to harass and oppress us.

John Eldredge explains:

> [Satan] suggests to us—as he suggested to Adam and Eve—some sort of idea or inclination or impression, and what he is seeking is a sort of "agreement" on our part. He's hoping we'll buy into whatever he's saying, offering, insinuating. Our first parents bought into it, and look what disaster came of it. But that story is not over. The evil one is still lying to us, seeking our agreement every single day.[5]

Our battle with "the powers of this dark world and against the spiritual forces of evil in the heavenly realms" begins with a fight to recognize and refuse their lies (Eph. 6:12).

Paul warns us, "Do not give the devil a foothold" (Eph. 4:27). Our ideas, even more than our sins, give the enemy a beachhead in our lives. Things may start subtly, with mental doors that are open just a crack. But, if given the chance, evil will wedge its foot in and eventually push the door wide open.

I just got off the phone with a woman in anguish. Under heavy fire spiritually, she is desperate to find deliverance from demonic harassment. The warfare she is under is extreme. She is besieged by obscene thoughts and hounded relentlessly by demonic voices. The voices berate her and viciously abuse her with the message that she is filthy, unlovable, and hopeless. She has already hit rock bottom, turned to chemicals for an emotional crutch, sacrificed her health, lost custody of her children, had a mental breakdown, and been locked away in a mental facility several times.

Without emotional affect, she feels like a human husk; empty, hollow, and devoid of any emotion, other than despair. It has been years since she has felt near to the love of God— even though she was once active in a vibrant ministry. Now, she makes the rounds, seeking out ministers, counselors, and anyone else who can help. Yet, she can't find relief.

She hasn't found freedom because, like Eric, she agrees with the lies. They feel true, therefore, she believes them to be true. The worse her situation gets, the easier it is for her to believe the lies. The more isolation and pain she feels, the easier it becomes to lose all hope. She can't imagine anything different, and she won't consider that God sees her in a different light.

Now evil has the upper hand. Every disappointing experience gives the devil another opportunity to say, "*See, I told you, nothing good will ever happen to you.*" Any time she risks sharing the level of harassment she is under, evil repeats the same old lie, "*You better not tell anyone what is going on. They will think you are crazy. You are hopeless.*"

Even though her situation is extreme, leading to a mental breakdown, the enemy's tactics are the same for her as for anyone else. Evil bombards her with ideas that she isn't good enough, that she is unlovable, that she is on her own, that God doesn't care enough to help, and that her life is utterly hopeless.

Satan is proposing those same kinds of lies to us all right now.

The good news is that her road to recovery is the same as ours. Her process may take longer, and she may need to dig deeper, but the way forward is still the same.

She needs what we all need. She needs to believe the story that God is telling about her life.

Reframing the Desert Season

The events that happen in our lives matter, but the way we interpret those events often matters more. Put another way, our problems aren't really the problem. It is what we think about our problems that is the real problem.

When challenges come in life (and they always do), the story we believe will make all the difference. If we believe that we are defeated and that life is hopeless, then every setback will reinforce this defeatist narrative.

For example, I recently worked with Adam, a brilliant man —one of the most gifted and tenacious people I have ever met. Intelligent, talented, disciplined, and driven, when he gave his life to Jesus, he gave God his all. An inspiring presence to be around, he lives a life sold out for Christ.

Everyone recognized Adam's hunger and talent. People often praised his clever ideas and strong work ethic. For years, people encouraged him by telling him that God would surely do great things in his life. He believed it. He has always had a vision to make a big impact.

Yet, with all his talent, hard work, and faithful devotion, Adam had yet to see some great destiny materialize. We met when he was in his mid-thirties. The threat of emotional and financial bankruptcy loomed heavily like a dark thunderstorm on the horizon. Broke and feeling like he was barely treading water, life didn't appear to be working out. Discouragement bombarded him daily.

Obsessed with trying to figure out why his life wasn't working, he asked:

"What am I doing wrong?"
"Am I blowing it?"
"Did I hear God's call wrong?"
"Is God holding out on me?"
"Am I a failure?"

Doubts and fears crept in. The devil whispered lies into his already tense and tumultuous inner dialogue:

> *"You need to try harder. Get it together!"*
> *"You're crazy for believing God will ever do something with your life."*
> *"You missed it!"*
> *"Why don't you just give up?"*
> *"You're a loser. You've already lost."*

Finally, came the clincher: *"You're washed up. God is done with you. You blew it. You missed your chance, and now your life is over. Just end it already."*

By this point, it was a battle to do anything more than wallow in self-pity. Full of doubts, this man of conviction now felt distant from God and alone in his pain. Satan was working overtime to discourage him. His difficult circumstances gave the devil plenty of material to work with.

Once full of promise, Adam now felt hopeless and alone in a hostile wilderness. He wondered if God had abandoned him to die in the desert of lost dreams. Satan was saying so. His life experiences seemed to be agreeing.

Yet, God had a different story to tell.

As we sat together, meeting to process what God was doing in his life, another narrative emerged. God showed us a different way to interpret Adam's current challenges. We started asking a new set of questions:

> *"What if you haven't screwed up your life and God hasn't forgotten about you?"*
> *"What if this desert season really is a part of God's plan?"*
> *"What if the changes taking place inside of your heart are important to the future God has in store for you?"*
> *"What if this wilderness road is actually the path to the Promised Land?"*

We did some hard work to discover and discard the old ideas that fueled his despair. I asked Adam to get quiet, center himself, and verbalize all the harsh internal messages he heard. We wrote them out on a whiteboard. One by one, we examined the thoughts, asking God if they were true. Together, we wrestled with his inner dialogue and took his thoughts captive to the truth.

Much of what Adam believed about himself wasn't true. Like many of us, he was too hard on himself. He, therefore, assumed that God must be hard on him too. With that mindset, he often felt like a failure. Of course, Satan was right there, ready to highlight every little mistake.

Yet, the weight of the shame, blame, and failure that came from that toxic narrative was too much to bear. Truly, it wasn't something God ever wanted Adam to bear. Nor does God want any of His children to languish under that weight. Everything changed when Adam let go of that burden.

He listened to a new narrative. He perked up. Adam's eyes got brighter. He set new goals—ones that focused more on his character than his achievements. He resumed hobbies and interests that he had abandoned years ago. He pursued God on a deeper level. He soon encountered God in exciting, fresh ways. New opportunities for work and travel appeared.

Life took on new meaning for Adam. He saw his circumstances differently. A new life story emerged. For the first time in years, he let go of anxiety and experienced inner peace.

The challenges in his life didn't go away overnight. In fact, Adam had several more obstacles to face. However, his ability to face those challenges changed dramatically.

He no longer saw his season in the desert as a punishment for failure, or as a sign that he had somehow screwed up. He no longer felt like God had forgotten him. He lived with a new confidence that God was guiding him through the desert, and into a land of promise.

He even embraced his recent challenges with a sense of

accomplishment. Having braved the wilderness, he now felt closer to Jesus, who also spent a challenging season in the desert. It bolstered Adam's faith to look over his own trials and see how God was guiding him forward.

Adam went from believing the devil's narrative to interpreting his life from a heavenly perspective. He traded in a hopeless, depressed mentality for a dynamic story that brought him new life.

He was just about to give up. Now Adam is out living a new adventure with God. The last time we spoke, he told me about one of his latest escapades snorkeling off the coast of a beautiful island beach.

Adam's gone from looking for an oasis amidst a spiritual desert to living on a tropical island. He traded in a tired, old story for a new and better one.

We should too.

FOUR

God's Truth & Your Identity

You are not what you think you are. There is a glory to your life that your Enemy fears, and he is hell-bent on destroying that glory before you act on it.

John Eldredge

Then you will know the truth, and the truth will set you free.

John 8:32

IT WAS MY LAST YEAR IN SEMINARY. AS PART OF MY MINISTRY training, I spent the summer volunteering as a hospital chaplain. I spent my days walking the halls, going from room to room, offering prayers, support, and a listening ear wherever I could.

It was tedious and challenging work, but also rewarding. I always got to witness God in action—comforting, consoling, helping, and healing the wounded and brokenhearted. There were many memorable encounters. But there is one patient who I will always remember.

I prepared to make my last patient visit for my shift. I

knocked, waited, then walked into the room. I took a deep breath as I plunged in.

I never knew what to expect when I walked into a patient's room. Sometimes people were sleeping, the medication in the IV drip having served its purpose. Often, I would encounter frantic family members, full of the angst that comes when one feels overwhelmed, powerless, and afraid.

This time I encountered a man who appeared to be the very definition of defeat. His shoulders slumped in quiet resignation; his very being screamed how pitiful and wretched he felt. It was obvious he had given up hope a long time ago.

The room felt stifling; so hard to breathe. Along with the thick air of hopeless resignation that wafted from him like thick dark clouds, there was something that felt more like a spiritual smog. It was oily, thick, and gray. It made the air heavy around him.

We made small talk. I asked him what brought him to the hospital. He confessed that it was alcohol poisoning. He had landed in the hospital by drinking himself into a dangerous stupor. It wasn't the first time. He was a repeat offender, having been in the same hospital, same room even, just a few weeks before.

His drinking had gotten out of hand. It had gone so far beyond a mere crutch to get through life. Now alcohol threatened to kill him. He seemed to invite death, longing for an end to his misery. Not willing to kill himself, he instead opted for slow suicide in a bottle.

Hungover and hopeless, he humbly shared about the mess his life had become. The desire to look good was long gone. Alcohol had dissolved that false pride. He disclosed to me—stranger though I was—the mistakes he made with his children, with his wife. All of them were no longer on speaking terms. He was on his own; excommunicated from his family and living from a bottle.

Up to this point, I had heard this story before. Over the

years, I have talked with thousands of people struggling with addictions. Their stories are often the same. Yet, somehow, this man stood out to me. Something about him seemed different. It was like God had highlighted him, encouraging me to give him special attention.

The man told me more. He told me of a time before his drinking became a downward spiral. He told me a story about a life where he was well off, happily married, healthy, and fit. He shared about how he was once a committed father who enjoyed a great relationship with his kids. He used to have a close relationship with God. Once upon a time he had even been an active leader in a thriving ministry.

That was all gone now. The story he told me about bygone days didn't match the man who sat before me. I wasn't sure I believed him. It seemed too far-fetched to believe that his life had ever been more than a train wreck. I couldn't reconcile his story with the evidence before me.

Oddly, it bothered me throughout the night. I kept thinking about him. I wondered how I might help, if I could even help. I wasn't sure I could do anything. Honestly, he needed a miracle.

Early the next morning, I felt God bring him to mind once again. So, in my quiet time, I asked for wisdom on how I might help this man. Hoping for just a trickle of insight, it caught me by surprise when God turned on the firehose of revelation.

God hit me with a deluge of information that affirmed this man's identity. He poured out words of purpose and meaning. The Lord told me that the man's story was indeed true. In fact, there was more that he had been too modest to share.

God called him a great man; a man created to lead. God created him to be a strong leader, a good husband, and a loving father. He had a powerful ability to coach others—both youths as well as adult men. The Lord intended for him to become a role model to the men in his community, someone the younger men could look up to. God called him into ministry. He destined this man to be a beacon of virtue and strength, someone who would make an impact in his community. I wrote everything that I heard the Lord speak. I knew God wanted me to share it with my patient.

It was a powerful experience for me to hear the Lord's affirmations. However, I still had a hard time believing what I heard God say. It just didn't seem to fit the reality of the man I met the day before. Regardless, I decided to share what I felt God had said.

I went to visit my patient again. When I entered the room, the thick air of gloom assailed me once again. The stale hopelessness still hung in the air. Sunlight poured in through the window, yet the atmosphere felt sickly and gray.

The man, too, seemed gray. Still pasty, his complexion looked similar to the color of dried mud. He was still in a stupor, too depressed to move. He sat on the edge of his bed, staring blankly at the wall. He didn't give any sign that he even saw me enter the room. I cleared my throat and said hello. He never even blinked.

I wondered if he could hear me, if he was mentally present at all. Even so, I told him everything I'd been feeling since the last visit. I told him I had been praying for him. I told him I believed God had told me things about him. I asked if I could share what I heard. Without the slightest trace of enthusiasm, he solemnly agreed.

I read what God had revealed to me that morning. I told him how God created him to be a powerful leader, a godly man, a family man. I told him how God made him to minister to others. He was destined to make a difference in his community.

It only took a few minutes to read my notes. In that brief span of time, everything changed. When I finished, a gust of wind rushed away from the man with a mighty, loud "*whoooosh.*" It seemed as if some force was just violently expelled from the man. The negative air that clung tightly to him, weighing him down, was cast out by words of truth. A sudden breeze came off of his chest, darted across the room, and passed right through the wall out of the building. On its way out, the gust of air knocked over a pile of papers and scattered them across the floor.

Taken aback, I looked over at the man to see how he was.

Remarkably, he seemed to be an entirely unfamiliar man. It was as if someone had switched my dejected patient for a leaner, cleaner, stunt double. He was altogether a different person. His eyes were no longer glazed over. His wilted posture disappeared. Instead, he stood tall and straight. He appeared to be a man with a message to share—a message you want to make time to hear.

His stupor gone, he now appeared to ponder deep thoughts. After a few moments of silence, he said, "*I'm different.*" It was the epitome of understatement. I answered, "*Yeah, you are!*" with all the wide-eyed wonder of a man who had just witnessed a miracle.

He took another moment to mull it all over. He said, "*I will check myself out of the hospital now. I think I am ready to leave.*"

I asked what he planned to do. He said he would go home and try to fix his marriage. He was ready to give up drinking. Ready to get his life back on track.

Over the years, I have heard many people say things just like that. Sadly, I am often skeptical. After hitting a new bottom, many people promise to quit drinking and change. While some do, most don't. This time, I knew a true change had happened.

A few minutes before sharing the words given by God, he was utterly hopeless—a shell of a man. Something lifted off of him. Some invisible weight was just exorcised from his life. He stood before me, a new man, a revived man. He was every bit the man that God had said he was.

I knew that he would leave the hospital that day and never

return. God set him free to live the life destined for him. God revealed the truth about his identity.

The truth had set him free.

The Truth Will Set Us Free

Truth is a weapon in spiritual warfare. It is both our best offense and our best defense.

Jesus said, "you will know the truth, and the truth will set you free" (John 8:32). He meant it.

That day in the hospital, the truth set my patient free. He listened to the words of God—words that restored his identity and reoriented his trajectory in life. Truth cut through the dark fog that kept him from the light.

Our spiritual battles always require truth.

Some people treat spiritual warfare as if power is the key. They scream at demons. They literally whack them out of people by administering a blow from the Bible upside some-one's head. It is quite a production—a showy affair. For all the hype, however, I doubt it is very effective.

We don't have to make a big scene, puffing ourselves up with imaginary spiritual power to combat the enemy. Anderson counters this myth, explaining how truth is far more effective than brute force:

> Freedom from spiritual conflicts and bondage is not a power encounter; it's a truth encounter. Satan is a deceiver, and he will work undercover at all costs. But the truth of God's Word exposes him and his lie. His demons are like cockroaches that scurry for the shadows when the light comes on. Satan's power is in the lie, and when his lie is exposed by the truth, his plans are foiled.[1]

Spiritual warfare doesn't require a lot of fluff and fanfare. You can scream at demons if you want to, but you don't have to. There is nothing wrong with the enemy's hearing. Your normal voice will work just fine.

Sometimes there are some true spectacles, physical manifestations of the enemy, but those are rare. True power encounters are even more rare. They tend to happen more often when people go looking for them.

For the most part, in almost any situation we find ourselves in, spiritual warfare is a matter of applying the truth. We counter the enemy's lies with the truth of God. The truth sets us free.

When a person under attack holds fast to the truth, the warfare will lift from their life. Sometimes it happens in an instant, like it did that day in the hospital. Sometimes it is more of a process. In either case, the more we accept and apply God's truth, the freer we will become.

A Stolen Voice

Amelia's story is all too common. Despite being brilliant, well educated, and wise beyond her years, she struggled to speak up, to share in social settings.

Amelia grew up believing the lie that no one wanted to hear anything she had to say. It silenced her as a child. As an adult, it felt impossible for her to say how she really felt. Even in private conversations, she had trouble speaking up and sharing her thoughts.

When we first met, she had incredible difficulty speaking. It wasn't just that she was shy—she actually had physical difficulty speaking up. Her throat would close up, preventing her from making a sound.

To her credit, she kept trying. She resisted the impulse to shut down and be quiet. Believing that God wanted to use her to help others, she kept trying to speak up.

That is when the real battle began.

We were sitting at a table, talking. Amelia opened her

mouth to say something but couldn't. Her eyes became as big as basketballs as she felt an invisible claw grasp her throat. She was trying to speak but it was impossible. Some invisible spiritual force had grabbed her throat and was squeezing it shut!

I calmly and quietly commanded the hand to let her go. No need to scream (misusing my voice wouldn't help her reclaim her own).

The claw let go.

The sensation quickly passed. Yet, the event left a lasting impact. It brought home the gravity of the situation. Amelia's inability to speak was more than just shyness or nerves. It was spiritual. Some foul spirit was actively trying to shut her up.

As it turns out, Amelia has an amazing ability to speak. God designed her with a prophetic gifting. She is a great public speaker, with a godly message to share with others. Her voice points people back to God. She has an incredible way of changing the course of a conversation with just a few words. She can also give voice to other people's feelings when they can't find the words to express themselves.

So, the devil had a reason to keep Amelia from speaking. By shutting her up, he silenced the flow of God's wisdom spoken through her.

His first line of attack came when she was young. Lying spirits whispered toxic narratives that discouraged her from ever speaking up.

"You aren't very smart."
"You don't have anything good to contribute."
"There is no point in saying anything. Somebody else will say it better than you ever could."
"Their thoughts are more valuable than yours."
"Keep quiet. Nobody will understand you anyway."
"Nobody wants to hear anything you say."

She listened to these lies when she was just a child.

Believing that she had nothing worthwhile to say to anyone, she just kept quiet.

When Amelia and I challenged the lies by pressing forward, engaging the struggle to speak up, the devil retaliated. The more she leaned into God's leading to speak, the more aggressively the devil struck back. He even went to bodily lengths to choke the words right out of her.

You might wonder how believing the enemy's lies could lead to something like a physical manifestation where the enemy has the power to affect someone's body. Author Timothy Warner sheds light on this kind of experience, "Satan's primary tactic is deception or clever lying, and the degree to which we believe any of his lies and come under the influence of deception is the degree to which Satan or demons have control of our lives."[2]

This is exactly what happened to Amelia. Her experience shows how believing a lie—agreeing with the devil's narrative—gave the enemy grounds to suppress her God-given ability to speak. Her physical experience of being choked came because she allowed her voice to be spiritually silenced and suppressed for so long.

I have seen this kind of thing happen with other people. God gifts some of us with a message to share and a unique ability to represent His heart to the world. Satan recognizes the gift. At an early age, evil launches an assault on these people's hearts, working hard to convince them to keep quiet. When they finally try to live a new story, to take a step toward reclaiming their God-given voice, a demonic hand tries a last-ditch effort to literally squeeze their throat and force them back into silence. It is a bullying power play that reveals the devil's desperation.

Ironically, the assault affirms the value of their words. After all, if it were true that they had nothing worthwhile to say, and that nobody wanted to hear it, why would the powers of hell work so hard to keep them quiet? Why silence someone unless their words truly have value?

If this ever happens to you, take it as confirmation that God has given you something good to say, and that the devil wants to shut you up. Press in, resist the devil, and share what God puts on your heart.

Happily, Amelia found her voice. She led her entire family into a freer, fuller life. Then she found a new calling, pursuing ministry training to help others. Scripture came true in her life: "When she speaks, her words are wise, and she gives instructions with kindness" (Prov. 31:26). Now she is using her voice to help other women reclaim the lives God created for them.

Eternal Identities

You are more than you think you are. There is an inherent glory to your life—to your very being—that is both prized by heaven and hated by hell.

God designed every single human being on purpose for a purpose. He destined each of us to make an eternal impact on the world.

God was also very intentional when He designed our personalities. He created each of us, quirks and all, on purpose. It is a marvelous mystery, but it is true. God designed you the way He did, simply because He likes you.

Read that again: God likes you. The real you. Not the made up you. Not the you that you try to be on Sunday morning. Nor the false self we all learn to put on at a young age. Certainly not the tarnished broken identity that the enemy tried to force upon you.

God likes the real you. He likes your quirky personality, and He enjoys spending time with you.

He likes you so much that He created you with eternity in mind. He wants to spend all the time in the universe hanging out with you. And now, He will stop at nothing to rouse your heart, call you out of the dominion of darkness, and awaken the light within you. "Awake, O sleeper, rise up from the dead, and Christ will give you light" (Eph. 5:14 TPT).

Unique as we are, the light of God shines through us differently. Like a prism, His light shines through the Church in a myriad of exciting colors. He made it so. He formed the Body of Christ from an eclectic band of colorful characters, every one unique, each eternally glorious.

God made each one of us to shine brightly and uniquely for all eternity. The truest thing about you isn't your sins, or your past, or your scars. The truest thing about you is the eternal identity that God has given you.

Within each of us, perhaps buried under years of baggage and unbelief, is an eternal identity, given to us by God. Our life on Earth, in a fallen state, is relatively brief. It is but a vapor in the context of all time and space (James 4:14).

However, you won't end when your life expires. You—the real you—will live forever. You are an eternal being. God made the very essence of who you are to last for all eternity. That is your true identity. The person God designed you to be for all eternity is your true self.

The life we have lived, burdened by sin, pain, and the damning lies of evil, isn't who we truly are. Not in Christ. The truest thing about you isn't where you have been, but where you are going. He has made a way forward; a way back to our true selves, back to our eternal identities. You are going to shine with ever-increasing glory for all eternity (2 Cor. 3:18).

God doesn't make junk. Quite the opposite; God makes epic beings. Consider what C. S. Lewis said in *The Weight of Glory*:

Remember that the dullest and most uninteresting person you talk to may one day be a creature which, if you saw it now, you would be strongly tempted to worship, or else a horror and a corruption such as you now meet, if at all, only in a nightmare... There are no ordinary people. You have never talked to a mere mortal. Nations, cultures, arts, civilization—these are mortal, and their life is to ours as the life of a gnat. But it is immortals whom we joke with, work with, marry, snub, and exploit—immortal horrors or everlasting splendors.[3]

Eternity will reveal our hearts. Then we will be known as we really are— splendid beings perpetually reflecting the glory of God or nightmarish horrors bent on the destruction of all that is good.

If you are a Christian, then you are a splendor in the making. Your heart is good. Even now, it is being purified— restored to its intended design. God is hard at work in you. His glory is aching to burst forth and shine through you.

God has given His people wonderful gifts and personalities. We are His instruments of bringing His goodness into the world. We are the agents of His restoration to the world. God wants us to shine. He destined us to make the world a better place.

When we live out of our eternal identity—when we manifest our true and God-given selves—we bless the world around us. Our personal uniqueness is an asset that benefits others (1 Cor. 12:7).

With His Spirit leading us from the inside, we bring His presence into atmospheres around us and no force of the enemy can stop the advance of the Church. We can trample the gates of hell underfoot as we take territory from the enemy and restore it to the kingdom of our Lord (Matt. 16:18). The Church, the people of God, will displace evil and carry the presence of God into the world.

That is our eternal destiny.

Identity Theft

Satan fiercely opposes the kingdom of God. He won't simply step aside and make room for the Body of Christ to do its thing. Just as he opposes God, the devil opposes each of us as well.

Yet, as Graham Cooke reminds us, "The enemy knows he doesn't have to beat the church, just deflect her from her own God-given destiny."[4] Satan took on the powers of heaven before, and lost. Now, instead of a direct power struggle, the devil uses his deceptive powers to steer us off course. This deflection from our God-given destiny comes in many forms: distraction, temptation, harassment, bullying, etc. Yet, while the tactics may differ from time to time, the core is always an attack on our identities.

Every spiritual assault is an attempted identity theft.

Satan wants to rob you of your God-given identity. The forces of darkness don't want you to know who you really are. They want you to play small and live small. The devil wants to render the Church impotent. He aims to convince each of us that we are weak, broken, helpless, hopeless, alone, and unable to make a difference.

Yet, it is our destiny to make a difference. We are Christ's hands and feet. We shine the light of God into the darkness. We carry His presence with us, and we spread His kingdom around us. We each have work to do—God gave every one of us a purpose, a unique blessing that only we can offer the world.

Nevertheless, how many believers do you know who live with a sense of purpose and passion? Be honest. How many moments have each of us squandered by giving into the belief that we have nothing to offer?

Satan doesn't want you to live the life that God created you for. The devil seeks to rob you of the life that God dreams for you. He would prefer that we spend our lives languishing in a prison of condemnation. He relentlessly attacks your heart to steal, kill, and destroy your identity, plus rob you of your destiny.

When we lose heart, when we fail to embrace our eternal identity, the devil doesn't even have to oppose us. If Satan can convince us to play small, to live limited and powerless lives, then he has won the battle before it has even begun. We will have done the devil's job for him.

Settling for a Lesser Story

Sometimes the simplest way for Satan to steal your destiny is to convince you to settle for less. Often, we settle for the scraps of life. We set our sights too low, seeking the shallow, and failing to pursue the things that have lasting value.

Sadly, the Church does the same thing. We have watered down the power of the gospel. We have settled for scraps of the Good News. Too often, the Church has reduced the power of holiness down to a belief that behaving ourselves is the highest virtue. As a result, we never step out of line. We become terrified of making mistakes, so we live buttoned up lives devoid of any real passion. Our repression leads us to settle for closet addictions instead of living from the courage of our convictions.

Yet, being a Christian is so much more than behaving yourself. In fact, it often means quite the opposite. Jesus had a way of defying expectations and acting outside of the status quo.

We are meant for more than mediocrity. We have a God-given light inside us. It's meant to shine (Matt. 5:16). When we opt for a lesser version of ourselves than God desires, we settle for less than God's best. How can we settle for spiritual scraps, when Christ offers us an abundant and fulfilling life?

When we forsake who we are, we allow Satan to steal our true identity. The enemy uses his words to tear us down and lead us astray. The devil is the supreme narcissist abuser. And, like every abuser, he pours out lies designed to tear us down and rob us of any hope we have for a better life. He tries to make us smaller, so his power can grow bigger.

The forces of hell couldn't be more pleased than when we live our lives as if we don't really matter. What threat does a sad, boring, and bland soul pose to the kingdom of darkness?

Sadly, the devil has infected our theology too with a version of Christianity that is far from good news. Twisting true humility, Satan tells us not to be who we are. He lies that it is better to hide our hearts and deny those God-given dreams within us.

But don't be confused. A godly humility doesn't make us smaller—it makes God bigger. Any gospel that keeps us silent and small isn't good news at all.

The apostle Paul had harsh words for the Galatian church after they set aside the gospel of freedom in favor of the scraps of legalism:

> I am shocked that you are turning away so soon from God, who called you to himself through the loving mercy of Christ. You are following a different way that pretends to be the Good News but is not the Good News at all. You are being fooled by those who deliberately twist the truth concerning Christ.
>
> Let God's curse fall on anyone, including us or even an angel from heaven, who preaches a different kind of Good News than the one we preached to you. I say again what we have said before: If anyone preaches any other Good News than the one you welcomed, let that person be cursed. (Gal. 1:6-9)

Evil works hard to sell us on a lesser gospel; one that convinces us to play small and settle for less. Instead of freedom, we settle for rules. Instead of a life ablaze with holy fire, we settle for lukewarm behavior modification. Thus, we can't help but focus on ourselves, our faults, and our failures. When the gospel of redemption becomes smaller, our sins seem so much bigger. We lose sight of our eternal identities and we settle for a worn-out adage like "*I am simply a sinner saved by grace.*"

The enemy is the author of this toxic narrative that focuses more on our failures than on the power of God to restore. The evil one lies and tells us we are disappointments to God, filthy sinners barely tolerable to our Lord.

How many Christians do you know who continue to struggle under the weight of toxic narratives like these?

> *"You are a disappointment to God."*
> *"God may love you, but He is really disgusted by your behavior."*
> *"You deserve this burden. It's punishment for your sins."*
> *"Your heart is wicked. You're dirty, broken, and full of sin."*
> *"Your dreams don't matter. They will only lead you astray."*
> *"You can't trust your feelings. Bury them deep."*
> *"Your heart doesn't matter."*

These thoughts are toxic. They are pure lies and don't come from God.

When we listen to these lies, we can't help but hide. Yet, when we hide who we really are—our true selves—we end up diminishing the light of God shining through us.

Yet, who can shine the light of God, if not us? Only the people of God, in a vibrant relationship with God, can shine the light of God. Only the Church, awake to its identity and destiny, can radiate Christ to the world.

Therefore, we desperately need to see our lives through God's eyes. We need a heavenly perspective. We need to know that we are sons and daughters of the King. We aren't orphans, on our own, left to fend for ourselves (John 14:18).

God loves you and wants you. He hasn't deserted you, and

He isn't the cause of your pain. Despite what the surrounding warfare is trying to tell you, God is for you, and His love is bigger than the lies coming against you (Rom. 8:31).

Truly, God loves you, and He likes you. He wants more for you than you can imagine. He is always working for your good. Right now, He is relentlessly pursuing you. He wants to see you come alive and live the life that He dreams for you.

We need this kind of heavenly perspective. We need to hold on to truth so we can overcome the challenges and condemning narratives that we face. We need the truth of God to transform how we see ourselves, life, and the world around us.

We need a new story. We need a God-sized story.

A God-Sized Story

Many people throughout Scripture resisted their calling. Moses argued with God, Jonah ran from Him, Jacob literally wrestled with God throughout his life. Others, like Saul, Paul, Peter, Gideon, and Zachariah, continued to fight, deny, and run from God's plan for their lives.

Why? Probably because they were listening to the wrong voice.

They listened to the voices inside that kept telling them to play small, that they were nobodies. But, if God believes in someone, then who are they to deny it?

Since God believes in you, who are you to deny it?

God believes in you because He sees something in you that you might not see. He knows how He made you. He knows your true identity. He knows your destiny.

Our destinies are defined by who we are, not by what we have done. What we do flows out of who we are. Consider this, a fruit tree is still a fruit tree regardless of whether or not it has ever born fruit. It is still an apple tree, even if it has not yet sprouted apples. It doesn't suddenly become a pine tree. Its design is still the same, regardless of its current situation. It is defined by what it was created to do, not what it has done.

Just like the fruit tree, your calling is defined by who you are, not what you have done up to this point in your life. Even if you haven't yet born fruit, you are still the person God says you are. You are still destined for something great—something God-sized. Whether or not you have seen fruit manifest yet isn't the point. The point is that you must begin to believe the story that God says is true.

It doesn't matter what anyone else thinks. It doesn't even matter what we think. It only matters what God says is true.

Gideon was a mighty warrior, though he was too afraid to see it (Judg. 6:11-23). Moses was a great leader—the greatest in Israel's history—despite his meek temperament and stutter (Exod. 4:10-17, Num. 12:3). God destined David to be king, though no one who knew him could see it. Not even the great prophet Samuel could recognize what God saw in David (1 Sam. 16:1-13). Even Jesus didn't seem like much from the world's point of view (Isa. 53:1-3). Yet, we all know how that story turned out.

God often hides great glory in unassuming packages. Yet, one day all will be revealed. The curtain will be pulled back, and the Lord will reveal to the entire world who we truly are. When the Lord makes His appearance, "he will bring all that is hidden in darkness to light and unveil every secret motive of everyone's heart. Then, when the whole truth is known, each will receive praise from God" (1 Cor. 4:5 TPT).

We have a tendency to hear these words and focus on the negative things that will be exposed. But the Bible is clear that God will reveal the aspects of our lives that deserve praise. Since we are born again—made new in Christ—God isn't interested in exposing our hidden sins. After all, we already made an admission of guilt when we asked Him into our lives. So, our entire life stories are safe with God.

God is eager to show the world the wonder of who we are.

Instead of exposing our brokenness, He wants to reveal the glory within us. Thus,

> "We can all draw close to him with the veil removed from our faces. And with no veil we all become like mirrors who brightly reflect the glory of the Lord Jesus. We are being transfigured into his very image as we move from one brighter level of glory to another" (2 Cor. 3:18 TPT).

Of course, God sees the sin in our lives. But do we realize He also sees the hidden gold? He saw the courage hidden deep down in Gideon. He saw the fierce loyalty buried in Moses. He saw that David had a heart much like His own.

This is how He sees you. Made new in Christ, God focuses on the glory within you. Just as creation aches to see the children of God revealed (Rom. 8:19), so too does the Creator long to see His kids come alive in their eternal identities.

It is time that we let go of the tired, old stories that hold us back. Christ's redemption does more than just resurrect our bodies one day in the future. The new life He brings resurrects our true identities in the here and now.

It's time for you to live from a new story, even if it feels awkward at first. Let go of that judgement. Let go of the past. Step into your future. Embrace your eternal identity. Be your true self, even if no one else can see it yet.

Ultimately, it isn't important what the world thinks about us, what Satan says about us, or even what we think of ourselves—it is only important what God says is true about us. Whether the world ever finds us impressive, God believes in us and rejoices when we walk in our true identity.

Even the Apostle Paul (who had an impressive resume) had to come to a place where he no longer cared what anyone thought about him. He only cared how God saw him (1 Cor. 4:3-4). He quit measuring himself against others. He only wanted to hear God's evaluation of his life.

You need to hear what God says about you. If He believes in you, then who are you to argue with God?

God says that you are:

A new creation (2 Cor. 5:17)
Chosen by Him (Eph. 1:4-5)
Adopted into His family (Eph. 1:5)
A child of God (John 1:12)
Joined with Jesus Christ (1 Cor. 6:15, 17)
A friend of God (John 15:15)
Wonderfully made (Ps. 139:14)
Destined for good things (Eph. 2:10)
Graced with the Holy Spirit (Rom. 5:5)
Gifted to help others (1 Co. 12:7)
Made strong even in difficulties (2 Cor. 12:10)
Able to overcome evil (Rom. 12:21)
Meant to triumph over the enemy (Rev. 12:11)

God, and only God, knows who you really are. You are who He says you are. Even your own estimation of yourself falls short. You aren't your thoughts, your feelings, or your failures. Your sins are forgiven. Your ideas and emotions are fluid things that will shift and change. But who you are in Christ is for all eternity.

It is time for you to live out of your eternal identity, not your shortcomings.

It is time for you to embrace your true identity and live from a new narrative.

FIVE

Your Authority & The Armor of God

Power to resist the devil is not a gift given to a few special believers. It is the privilege and responsibility of every child of God.

Timothy Warner

Be strong in the Lord and in his mighty power. Put on the full armor of God, so that you can take your stand against the devil's schemes. For our struggle is not against flesh and blood, but against the rulers, against the authorities, against the powers of this dark world and against the spiritual forces of evil in the heavenly realms. Therefore put on the full armor of God, so that when the day of evil comes, you may be able to stand your ground, and after you have done everything, to stand.

Ephesians 6:10-13

I WANT TO TELL YOU A SPIRITUAL WARFARE STORY WHERE THE enemy won.

As we have already discussed, the devil does his best work while hiding in the shadows. However, sometimes the demonic realm will act in obvious, even over-the-top, ways. These overt manifestations usually come when the enemy is about to lose its hold over a person's life.

When someone is close to breaking a harmful agreement or discovering a demonic dynamic at work in their life, the enemy becomes desperate to maintain his power over a person. In those moments, "the snarling, wicked powers of darkness will do all they can to intimidate and frighten you."[1] This is all for show. Those frightening displays try to convince us that evil has more power than it truly does.

Sadly, in this story, that strategy worked.

Many years ago, when I was a fairly new Christian, I was ministering to a young man named Luke. He was in a rough spot. He was battling several addictions, trying hard to get a fresh start in life. Many times he made a good beginning, yet in every case, he would fall back into the same old cycle.

The source of his trouble was that he wouldn't break with his occult past. No stranger to sex, drugs, and rock 'n roll, he was once a practicing Satanist. As you would expect, worshipping darkness gave the enemy extra power over Luke's life.

We met several times. Over coffee, I shared with him what God had done in my life. I talked with him about my own struggles. We talked candidly about how he, too, needed to step away from his old life so he could find a new one. Truly, only Jesus could resurrect his life and bring beauty from the ashes of his past. As our conversations progressed, I was enthusiastic and felt that Luke was about to give his life to Christ.

I was unprepared for what happened in our last meeting.

Like we normally did, we met at a coffee shop. We grabbed drinks and went outside to talk privately. It was a bright, sunny day with no sign of foul weather.

Our conversation started pleasantly but took a dark turn rather quickly. As I asked him if he was ready to make a commitment to a new life, his face turned sour. He stared at his feet. In a sad, defeated tone, he said, "*I can't.*"

I asked, "*Why?*"

"*Because, they won't let me,*" was his dejected reply.

At first, his response confused me. I started to ask him what he meant. Before I could even get the words out, something happened. Then, I knew exactly what he meant.

A suffocating feeling of terror surrounded us. We were no longer alone. A cold, dark presence entered our conversation. It loomed menacingly. A slimy, icy feeling swept over us. I was immediately nauseated. I also had goosebumps, although we were standing in direct sunlight on a warm summer day.

Luke said, "*They are here.*"

Yeah. No kidding.

"*They won't let me go.*" He meekly apologized. "*I can't go with you.*"

I continued to minister to Luke, to tell him he didn't have to live like a slave to these spirits. He could go to Christ. Jesus would set him free anytime that he wanted.

As I talked, a ferocious wind picked up and drowned out my words. It was a terrible sound, like a roaring freight train. Nearly deafening, it was effective at silencing our conversation.

Being from the Midwest, I am familiar with tornadoes. They come on suddenly and sound like a runaway train. Naturally, I wondered if a tornado was coming close. Yet, as I looked around, the world was perfectly at peace. Not more than fifteen feet away from us, small groups of patrons continued to sip their coffee and enjoy the summer sun. Meanwhile, I was shouting at Luke, trying to make my voice heard, though he was only a foot away. This abnormal twister apparently centered solely on the two of us.

The wind picked up litter, hurling it our way. Caught in the air current, bits of trash circled around us. Leaves and other debris kept flying in my face.

Then, as if all of this wasn't enough, the surrounding fixtures shook. A nearby parking sign twisted and whipped furiously. I feared that at any moment it would tear free of the bolts that held it in place and come hurling toward us. No doubt it would make a damaging projectile in the hands of gale force winds.

This was all over the top. Who had ever heard of a localized mini tornado swirling around two people trying to talk about Jesus? It was all too clear that some dark force wanted to disrupt our conversation. Some demonic spirit had laid claim to Luke. It was now fighting to keep its hold on him.

As I talked about surrender to Christ, the enemy made a show of power. It was quite the performance. Evil was going to great lengths to sell the story that it was more powerful than God. This entire scene was an effort to sabotage Luke's opportunity to hear the Good News and choose Jesus.

The demonic demonstration made a strong impression on him. Bullied by this show of force, Luke capitulated and chose to believe the lie that evil was more powerful than God. Resigned to his fate, he agreed with the lie that he could never escape this life. Though he hated the cycle he was in, he surrendered to it.

He said, *"I have more power here on this side."*

With that, he turned and walked away. Our conversation was over.

I tried to talk with him a few times after that day. Sadly, he was no longer interested in talking with me. His mind was made up. Luke made his choice to stay in the enemy's kingdom.

He made his choice to stay in bondage to a life he hated.

Silencing the Wind

That was a long time ago. I was fairly new in my faith when I tried ministering to Luke. Since then, I have learned a few things.

If something like that were to happen again, I would

simply command it to stop. I don't tolerate those kinds of bullying distractions anymore.

The enemy often acts up when people are on the verge of salvation or when they are nearing some other breakthrough in their lives. Though sometimes dramatic and frightening, these displays of power are still just a show.

Luke was on the verge of dedicating his life to Christ. If he had persisted just a bit farther, it would have ended the whole dramatic distraction. I didn't know it back then, but it really doesn't take much to silence demonic manifestations. Usually saying something like, *"In the name of Jesus, I command you to stop"* is sufficient. Even just saying *"Stop"* is often enough.

Jesus also had an encounter with an unnatural, fierce wind. Much like my encounter, this one was also over the top, so much so that the disciples feared for their lives.

A storm with wild winds threatened to capsize their little fishing boat. Panicking, the disciples franticly roused Jesus. Notably, he couldn't have been calmer. Arising from His slumber, His serene response was simply to tell the wind, *"Quiet! Be still!"* (Mark 4:39). Unlike His disciples, the storm didn't rattle Jesus.

Christ often encountered evil spirits that made a dramatic scene. One day, while teaching in the synagogue, He encountered one that made a disruptive spectacle of itself. Again, He simply replied, *"Be quiet"* (Mark 1:25). Frequently, Jesus dealt with demonic beings by commanding them not to speak (Luke 4:41).

When we encounter overt spiritual warfare, or dramatic manifestations, we can follow Christ's example and tell the spirits to stop. Sometimes more work may be necessary to set a person free from bondage, but it might surprise you how effective it can be to just tell evil to stop and go away.

Silencing the Spirit of Suicide

Kelly and I were working through some deep issues. It was tough work, and she was confronting some difficult areas of trauma in her life. This was the first time she had ever confronted the pain of her past. She usually ran from it. But that strategy never works, the past always catches up to us.

Overwhelmed by painful feelings that she had repressed for years, she longed for an escape. Thoughts of suicide came to mind, and she couldn't shake free of them. She felt tempted to run from all the pain in one last move. It became a nagging thought that plagued her often, but, interestingly enough, never when she was at church or with her friends. The thoughts of ending it all only came when she was tired and alone.

The thoughts of death grew in intensity. They assaulted her regularly. They kept her up at night, hijacking her rest with dark and terrible images. Terrified constantly, she was both afraid of her feelings and that she might end her life.

We talked about her options. She was desperate to know what to do. We considered hospitalization. She was willing to go that far, as she really didn't want to die. She didn't want to act on these suicidal thoughts. Even so, they continued to plague her relentlessly.

That stood out to me. It was notable that she genuinely seemed to hate the intrusive thoughts. It made me question if they were actually her own. I suspected spiritual warfare was behind these dark thoughts.

I suggested that before she commit herself for hospitalization we try an experiment and command the suicidal thoughts to go away. She was skeptical. She had never considered these thoughts might come from spiritual warfare. Although doubtful it would do anything, she tried my suggestion anyway.

She said, *"In Jesus's name, go way. Leave me alone."*

And you know what? They did.

The thoughts left her at once. Suicidal thoughts never her plagued her like that again.

There were a few occasions when the demonic ideas tried to come back. Each time they did, though, Kelly stood her ground and told them again to leave. They always left. Now they are gone for good. Kelly is finally free to address the deeper issues in her life without these dark thoughts getting in the way.

Please don't think I mean to suggest that suicidal thoughts are something we should take lightly. I don't think that at all. Sadly, I have lost several friends to suicide. Nor do I think all mental health issues will go away because we command them to. Yet, I think it might surprise us how many serious issues would go away if we treated them like warfare.

John Eldredge, an experienced counselor, explains how this works:

> Maybe half the stuff people are trying to "work through" in counseling offices, or pray about in their quiet times, is simply agreements they've made with the Enemy. Some foul spirit whispers, I'm such a stupid idiot, and they agree with it; then they spend months and years trying to sort through feelings of insignificance. They'd end their agony if they'd treat it for the warfare it is, break the agreement they've made, and send the Enemy packing.[2]

There were a few things about Kelly's situation that implied spiritual warfare was involved. First, she hated the thoughts she was having. That was telling. It meant that the thoughts were intrusive, unwelcome, and in direct conflict with her heart's true desires. Second, the thoughts were distracting her from what God was doing in her life. While Jesus was guiding her deeper into healing for her past, these thoughts were driving her deeper into fear and pain. Third, the thoughts seemed to come upon her in vulnerable moments and never in the presence of trusted others, never in places dedicated to God. These were clues that suggested that Kelly was under spiritual attack.

When she finally took a stand, the warfare revealed itself for what it was, and then it was removed. Just as James proclaimed, she resisted the devil, and he fled from her (James 4:7).

Somewhere in her life, Kelly made an agreement with a lie that said she needed to run away from her feelings. It became her strategy to avoid facing the pain of her past. It seemed her issues were just too difficult to deal with. She believed that her pain was so great it would destroy her if she ever felt it. She agreed with the enemy that it was better to be numb and run away from her past. So, when all other attempts to run away failed, her last option was to end it all. It felt like the only way to finally be free of her pain.

When she finally faced the warfare, it set in motion a cascade of healing moments. The pain of the past lost its hold over her. Now she is recovering from a life lived in bondage to the wrong story.

God empowered Kelly, making it possible to live in wholeness and freedom on a level beyond anything she ever imagined was possible. Her true self is emerging. Her eternal identity is shining forth!

It is an awesome thing to behold.

Imparted Authority

Jesus did more than just save us from our sins, and salvation is more than just a ticket to heaven when we die. Jesus imparted the authority to spread His kingdom—to make the world a better place.

The work of Christ—His life, death, resurrection, and ascension—invites us into an entirely new life. It is an abundant life, where the Spirit of God flows out from within us (John 7:38). And His Holy Spirit within us is more powerful than any enemy we will ever encounter.

Jesus has, "all authority in heaven and on earth" (Matt. 28:18). Remarkably, He shares His authority with the members of His Body. Jesus gave His followers the ability to evict evil from the world around them.

On one occasion, Jesus commissioned seventy disciples to go out and spread the Good News of the kingdom. They preached, performed miracles, and cast out demons (Luke 10:1-23). They returned, full of excitement and enthusiasm, remarking, "Lord, even the demons submit to us in your name" (Luke 10:17).

Jesus responded, saying to His disciples, "I have given you authority to trample on snakes and scorpions and to overcome all the power of the enemy" (Luke 10:19). Like Jesus, the disciples had the authority to tell demons to take a hike. They fought spiritual battles simply by telling the enemy to flee.

The remarkable authority to cast out evil continues on with us. The same power of the Spirit that flowed through the disciples flows in us. Clinton Arnold, author of *3 Crucial Questions about Spiritual Warfare*, explains that "the authority to cast out demons is not only an authority exercised by Jesus or the twelve foundational apostles, but is passed on to others whom Jesus sends out to perform the mission that he calls them to undertake."[3]

When Jesus sends someone on a mission, He gives them the ability and authority to carry out the work. Where He calls, He also equips.

Evil can't stop the kingdom of God. The forces of darkness are never too powerful for the Spirit of God. In fact, the very gates of hell bend and break as the people of God advance His kingdom (Matt. 16:18).

The power of God within us is great. He never meant for us to live as helpless victims of the enemy. God destined us to live free, to make life better for all by overcoming and evicting evil from the world around us.

We are the Church; we are the powerful people of God. We are destined to shine.

Conquering Sheep

The disciples may not have looked like much to the outside world. People saw them as "unschooled, ordinary men" (Acts 4:13). Many were laborers before they met Jesus. Others had sketchy pasts. None of them were perfect. Even the best of them had serious flaws.

Yet, they commanded demons to depart. They carried the authority of heaven. They ventured into hostile spiritual territory, battling the dark forces they encountered. They returned victorious, celebrating how they had conquered evil spirits.

Lest they forget where the real power to overcome the enemy came from, Jesus reminded them that their restored relationship with God was the real reason to celebrate (Luke 10:18-20). The disciples conquered evil because the power of God was within them, and that power was greater than any threat that came against them.

Jesus sent His disciples out as "lambs among wolves," seemingly vulnerable to attack (Luke 10:2). Instead, they were destined to triumph.

In the same way, we, too, live in a spiritually hostile world. Yet, we are destined to overcome. You may not feel powerful. Like the disciples, you may not look like much on the outside. However, the power of God within you is mighty.

Strengthened by Christ's power and authority at work in you, you can do great things. By His power, you can drive the devil away.

You need to believe this. You need to own this. You need to choose the right story.

As Neil Anderson said,

Nothing is more foundational to your freedom from Satan's bondage than understanding and affirming what God has done for you in Christ and who you are as a result. We all live in accordance with our perceived identity... If you see yourself as the helpless victim of Satan and his schemes, you will live like his victim and be in bondage to his lies. But if you see yourself as the dearly loved and accepted child of God that you really are, you will live as a child of God.[4]

The people of God need to affirm the truth and live as the beloved children of God we are.

When evil acts up, we can listen to the devil's narrative, believing the lies that hold us in bondage. Or we can live from a different story. We can live like victors. God has made us "more than conquerors" (Rom. 8:37). Nothing, not the troubles of life nor the power of the enemy can separate us from the love of Christ our King (Rom. 8:37-39).

Author and preacher, A. W. Tozer once wrote, "The sheep need not be terrified by the wolf; they have but to stay close to the shepherd."[5] Indeed, our Good Shepherd walks with us through the Valley of Darkness, guarding us with His power and authority (Ps. 23:4). He anoints us—declaring His approval of our true identities—and celebrates with us, in the midst of our enemies (verse 5).

Like Paul, there may be times when the voice of fear says we are like sheep destined for slaughter (Rom. 8:36). Yet, no power of hell can separate us from the love of God. Through the power of His love, we are more than capable of conquering the strategies of Satan.

We are safe in God's hands.

You are Safe Here

Karen came in for a session with our ministry team. A little shy at first, slowly she opened up. Within a few minutes, she was leaning towards us, engaged, and openly sharing her struggles.

She told us about an issue she couldn't overcome. She wanted to share, to unload the burden she was bearing. She was ready to find freedom. She felt that spiritual warfare was a big part of her problem. She even reported that she regularly felt a shadowy presence looming over her.

Then, seemingly out of nowhere, in one violent moment, she went from leaning forward to being tossed backward. She hit the back of the sofa she was sitting on, and the wall behind it. It looked as if some invisible force had her pinned to the couch.

I can't begin to describe the look of terror in her eyes. Shocked into silence, the panicked look on her face desperately pleaded for help.

I was angry at the enemy. Fed up. I had had enough of him messing with the people I ministered to. I wasn't about to tolerate this kind of interruption.

Quietly, but firmly, I said, *"That is enough."*

Then, gently, I said to Karen, *"You are safe here."*

And that was that. It was over in an instant. The invisible force let go. She sat back down and regained her breath. After that, we had no more trouble from demonic manifestations for the rest of her session.

In God's care, she was safe. She didn't have to put up with demonic harassment any longer.

As we continued our conversation, Karen told us about other experiences where she had suffered spiritual attacks. Although they were similar manifestations, she had never experienced anything of this magnitude before.

Before she left our session, she knew she would never have to experience anything like that again. She no longer had to listen to a story that made her feel defeated, harassed, and unable to defend herself. God gave her a new story, one where she was in control of her own body and had the power to effect genuine change in her life.

Though she came into our session like a shy sheep, she left like a fierce lion.

Obstinately Standing Firm

Although I never tire of watching people find freedom, it does, however, get old watching people get harassed by the enemy. It upsets me. I get angry. When I get angry, I get obstinate.

Obstinacy is a kind of stubborn defiance. It causes you to dig in your heels and refuse to move. It makes a person unwaveringly committed to their course of action (even if it is the wrong one). Obstinacy isn't usually considered a good thing, but when it becomes a weapon in spiritual warfare, obstinacy is a glorious thing.

When our defiant obstinacy becomes dedicated to God, it becomes a powerful tool for His purposes. Holy obstinacy allows us to persevere and maintain single-minded focus in the face of trials (James 1:2-8). It keeps us committed to the purposes of the Lord, running the race laid out before us. Like Jesus, we can endure moments of suffering and shame, standing firm in our expectation of the joy to come (Heb. 12:2).

With a steadfast holy obstinacy, we can stand firm in the face of any attack the enemy sends our way. We need to stand firm. We need to resolutely face our foes with unwavering dedication to the story that God is telling.

Standing firm is a big deal. Often the only thing we need to do to win spiritual warfare is simply to resist the enemy. It is like James said, "Stand up to the devil and resist him and he will turn and run away from you" (James 4:7 TPT). In fact, standing up to the enemy—and standing firm—is the key point behind the famous spiritual warfare passage in Ephesians 6.

I am sure you are familiar with the verses. In these memorable lines, the apostle Paul compares our spiritual protection to an ancient suit of armor. Many Christians know these lines. They are undoubtedly the most well-known Bible verses regarding spiritual warfare.

We may know these words well, yet how easy is it for us to miss the point? The sole reason we are told to put on the armor of God is so we can stand up to the enemy; "Put on the full armor of God, so that you can take your stand against the devil's schemes" (Eph. 6:10).

This theme of standing firm is so critical to the passage that Paul repeats it several times:

> Finally, be strong in the Lord and in his mighty power. Put on the full armor of God, so that you can *take your stand against* the devil's schemes. For our struggle is not against flesh and blood, but against the rulers, against the authorities, against the powers of this dark world and against the spiritual forces of evil in the heavenly realms. Therefore put on the full armor of God, so that when the day of evil comes, you may be able *to stand your ground*, and after you have done everything, to *stand*. *Stand firm* then, with the belt of truth buckled around your waist, with the breastplate of righteousness in place, and with your feet fitted with the readiness that comes from the gospel of peace. In addition to all this, take up the shield of faith, with which you can extinguish all the flaming arrows of the evil one. Take the helmet of salvation and the sword of the Spirit, which is the word of God. (Eph. 6:10-17; emphasis mine)

When the enemy attacks us—either with dramatic demonstrations or whispered warfare—we have to stand up to him.

We can't just roll over and take the enemy's abuse. We must resist him.

You can resist him. You can fight evil, and you can win!

Don't allow the enemy to steal, kill, or destroy the things you love. Stand against evil's tyranny. Stand your ground!

You don't fight alone. Christ is with you. Christ is in you. Christ has given you victory.

The New Testament scholar Andrew Lincoln reminds us that, "the decisive victory has already been won by God in Christ, and the task of believers is not to win but to stand, to preserve and maintain what has been won."[6] We stand and fight to keep the victory that God has already won in our lives.

So, stand firm in your mission. Stand firm in your victory. Stand firm in your eternal identity.

Stand firm in the truth of God's story.

SIX

Experiencing Trouble & Living in Victory

Victory is not the absence of problems; it is having peace and joy in the midst of them. Victory is continuing to bear good fruit for the kingdom of God, even when we are going through difficulties. If we continue to worship and honor God, then no matter what the enemy brings against us, we will demonstrate our belief that God is working on our behalf and that we are confident He will bring us through our challenges victoriously.

Joyce Meyer

Our boast is in the Lord our God, who makes us strong and gives us victory! Our enemies will not prevail; they will only collapse and perish in defeat while we rise up, full of courage.

Psalm 20:7-8 TPT

I STARTED THIS BOOK TALKING ABOUT TROUBLE. I'M SURE IT IS something that we can all relate to. After all, life is hard. There is no way to escape that fact. It is good that we admit it, that we call it like it is.

Life is tough. Did you know that Jesus said as much? The

night before His crucifixion, He told his disciples, "In this world you will have trouble" (John 16:33). It was one of the last things He said. Straight and to the point. No sugar coating it. On His way to Gethsemane, Jesus laid His cards out on the table; *"Life in this world will sometimes be very tough."*

Boy, He wasn't kidding, was He?

I think about the troubles of life, like how it often feels like an uphill struggle and we have to battle just to get through another day. Bills, traffic, career, kids, health, family, finances—it can sometimes be so difficult. It is often more difficult than seems fair—and that is just the stuff of daily life. Add to that the problems facing the world: racism, riots, rhetoric, pandemics, politicians, propaganda, and perverted pastors.

It is often overwhelming and oppressive. So much fighting. So much trouble. Battles happening on every front.

None of us has to go looking for trouble; it generally has a way of finding us. While God's plans for you are good, life this side of heaven is still full of trials and tribulations.

Along with the troubles of life, we have a real adversary. Our enemy tirelessly "works to make life worse, not better."[1] We cannot forget this fact. Scripture reminds us we are engaged in a battle. It beckons us to remember where the real fight is:

> We're not waging war against enemies of flesh and blood alone. No, this fight is against tyrants, against authorities, against supernatural powers and demon princes that slither in the darkness of this world, and against wicked spiritual armies that lurk about in heavenly places (Eph. 6:12 VOICE).

God has good plans in mind for you. He dreams of good things to give you. Meanwhile, the devil works to make your life harder and more painful than it already is. His demonic minions attack your mind with thoughts designed to make your life worse in any way they can.

That is the real battle. Though life in the world can often feel like a battle, the real fight is with the invisible evil we can't see.

If we are to live well, we have to find victory over our enemy. We need to find a way to live free, even while life is still challenging. We need a spiritual victory that lasts, even through hard times.

Elijah's Battle

The spiritual life is more like a marathon than a sprint. Following Jesus isn't a one-time thing that happened years ago when we decided to let Him into our lives. We have to keep following Him.

Likewise, spiritual warfare isn't something we overcome once and for all either. It's not like we only have to fight one glorious battle, and then the warfare is all done for the rest of our time on Earth. The Old Testament prophet, Elijah, seemed to think so, and he was grievously disappointed.

You probably already know this story from 1 Kings. Elijah had an amazing experience on top of Mount Carmel. He won a tremendous victory over the evil prophets of the demon-god Baal. Fire fell from heaven. Rain poured down, breaking a seven-year drought. Israel rose up and destroyed the soothsayers who had led them astray (1 Kings 18:16-46).

It was an unbelievable day. An epic victory! Yet, while Elijah and the Israelites won the battle, the war continued on.

At the start of the next chapter, the evil queen, Jezebel, threatened to kill Elijah. Terrified, he fled to the wilderness and had a breakdown. He cried out, "I have had enough, Lord," and then, "take my life" (1 Kings 19:4 NLT). Elijah had spent everything he had in the battle. Now, exhausted and depressed, he was done.

Mercifully, God met Elijah in that broken place. He sent an angel to tend to him (1 Kings 19:5-7) and later gave the prophet another mountaintop experience. Yet, this revelation was different. Whereas the experience on Mount Carmel was a show of spiritual power, Elijah's experience on Mount Sinai gave him spiritual staying power.

God spoke to Elijah in a gentle whisper, a still, small voice that reminded him he wasn't alone. He called Elijah's attention back to his purpose; back to his story.

God spoke softly to the prophet's heart, reminding him not to give up. He reoriented Elijah's perspective and showed him he was never alone. There were other spiritual resistance fighters. In fact, seven thousand other Israelites never bowed a knee to Baal. They, too, stood firm and never gave in.

God then gave Elijah a new mission. He also gave him someone to mentor. He connected the prophet with Elisha, someone with whom he could share his experience, strength, and hope. The younger man desperately needed to hear his elder's frontline experience. Elisha would one day face his own battles; entire armies would show up at his door. He needed to know that God was with him, and that heaven's armies were greater than any threat he faced.

Elijah's life was full of ups and downs. He had an amazing supernatural ministry filled with hardships, challenges, and unfair treatment. However, as part of his reward, he got the unprecedented experience of being carried off to heaven in a chariot of fire.

Though Mount Carmel was a stunning spiritual victory, the real victory of Elijah's life was staying the course. He held onto the story that God would come through. He believed in a narrative which said that, eventually, God would deliver Israel. He remained steadfast to that story, standing firm and true despite all he faced. He clung to God through it all. His faithfulness was his greatest victory.

We, too, must cling to the right story. Trouble will come.

We will have days of victory, and we may also know defeat. There will be times where it feels like we just got knocked flat on our face. Life will be confusing at times. It will be hard to know which way is up and which way to go. There will be times when life doesn't seem fair or make any sense; times where our faith doesn't seem to work. Days where God is quiet. Dark days where it feels like evil is winning.

When those days come, dig your heels in with holy obstinacy. Know that you get to choose the narrative you listen to. Know that you get to choose the story you believe.

You don't have to agree with the lies that evil throws at you. You don't need to partner with every painful feeling. You get to choose your own story. No matter what battles may come your way, you always get to choose how you will meet them.

Fighting from Victory

Our war isn't over yet. The ultimate victory hasn't yet come. One day it will.

Oh yes! One day, Christ, the Risen King, will come with glory blazing like the sun. A sword in His hand, He will bring the final reckoning. He will be the devil's doom. All evil will be thrown down, judged, punished, and purged. Jesus will win the greatest, glorious victory, and it will be a time of magnificent celebration; a heavenly feast. Crying will cease. Pain, death, sin, and Satan will be no more. Heaven will finally reign.

We aren't there yet. It's not yet time for that final showdown.

Until then, we do the best we can. We must continue to "fight the good fight of the faith," while we wait for Christ to return (1 Tim. 6:12). We look forward to the day when God will finally make everything right. Until then, it is imperative we trust in His final victory.

Rest assured, we come out on top. We fight from the vantage of victory, knowing that our side will win in the end. We fight *from* victory, not *for* victory.

It may, at times, be hard to keep going. It may feel like a monumental effort to push past the false narratives and stand firm in the real story. There will be times that require hard work to believe the story that God is telling (John 6:29). Yet, even a small amount of faith can break through a mountain.

As life's battles continue to come our way, it is important we stay in the fight. We must do what we can to not grow weary or discouraged. We must lean into the truth that, "at the proper time we will reap a harvest if we do not give up" (Gal. 6:9). Truly, we will be rewarded for the trials we have endured (James 1:12).

David's Defeat

Christ's victory on the cross shows us the ultimate victory is coming. But the last battle hasn't yet begun. Until then, our outlaw enemy is still at large. Thus, we face a myriad of smaller battles—spiritual skirmishes—that we can't evade or ignore.

Nor can we afford to fool ourselves, thinking that we can fight spiritual warfare only for a season, then turn the battle over to others. Spiritual warfare isn't the kind of thing where you do your tour of duty and then retire. We can't kick off the shoes of peace, hang up the shield of faith, lay back in a spiritual La-Z-Boy, and call it good.

Spiritual battles don't go away just because we are tired of fighting them.

King David tried that. Look where it got him. In the time "when kings go off to war," he stayed home (2 Sam. 11:1). He wanted to relax in the comforts of his palace. David expected others to fight the battles for God's kingdom. Tragically, his reluctance to fight made him easy prey when temptation came his way.

David was a great man, a valiant and mighty warrior. Though a man after God's own heart, he made some disastrous choices in his personal life. Chief among them, he compromised his integrity and jeopardized his entire future when he slept with Bathsheba.

David knew better than to sleep with another man's wife. Yet, somehow, he believed a lying narrative that convinced him this adultery was a good idea. The evil one must have also been there on the roof the day that David's integrity failed; an invisible evil standing next to David, encouraging him to take a second look, to let his eyes linger, when he should have walked away.

Though David was responsible for his own actions, I believe he was under spiritual attack. Temptation slid in, and it caught him off guard.

Ironically, he wouldn't have even been in such a spot if he had gone off to war like the rest of his army. The spiritual attack ensnared him when he tried to avoid the wars the other kings were fighting. Had he engaged the battles before him, he wouldn't have fallen into sin with Bathsheba.

There is a lesson in David's story for all of us. As much as we may want to escape the challenges of life and the warfare that can feel so relentless, we can't ignore the battles that come our way.

And battles will come; trouble is still active in the world. Jesus warned us it would be this way. Yet, He also added, "Take heart! I have overcome the world" to remind us to have courage (John 16:33). While the challenges are real, no trial we face is greater than our God. Indeed, the power of God within us is greater than the evil in the world (1 John 4:4).

So, we cling to a victorious mindset, holding fast to the truth of our identity. We continue to face the trouble that comes our way, without ever losing hope.

The Power of Hope

In his book, *Man's Search for Meaning,* Jewish psychologist Viktor Frankl shares the horrors he endured as a prisoner in a Nazi concentration camp.

The Nazis ripped Frankl's life apart. His wife, mother, and father were all murdered in the camps. His life's work destroyed, he watched many of his friends die right before his eyes. He lost everything and everyone he loved.

The things Frankl survived defy imagination. He shared one story about a fellow prisoner who was having a terrible nightmare. He was about to wake the man up, but then realized the man was better off as he was.

> I wanted to wake the poor man. Suddenly I drew back the hand which was ready to shake him, frightened at the thing I was about to do. At that moment I became intensely conscious of the fact that no dream, no matter how horrible, could be as bad as the reality of the camp which surrounded us.[2]

During the Holocaust, evil had the upper hand. It was literally hell on earth. No nightmare that Frankl could fathom was worse than the reality he witnessed every day. Tragically, Frankl often saw his fellow prisoners die in gruesome ways. The Nazis used them as slaves. They intentionally worked the inmates so hard that they would collapse. They fell down, dead from exhaustion. The Nazis literally worked them to death. Countless starved, half-naked bodies piled up.

Ironically, Frankl found that being physically stronger or more fit didn't help a prisoner survive longer in the work camps. In fact, "some prisoners of a less hardy make-up often seemed to survive camp life better than did those of a robust nature."[3] Time and time again, the prisoners who survived the torture were the ones who found meaning and purpose despite their pain.

Purpose, not fitness, made the difference between life and death.

Frankl witnessed it time and again; those who lost hope perished. The prisoners who gave up their dreams for a better future became doomed. Above all else, his fellow prisoners needed hope if they were to survive their dehumanizing existence.

Fond of quoting Friedrich Nietzsche, Frankl wrote, "He who has a *why* to live for can bear with almost any *how*."[4] It was knowing their *why*, their reason to live, that enabled the Jewish prisoners to prevail over the nightmarish conditions.

For some, this sense of purpose meant holding onto the hope of seeing their loved ones again. Others thought about the books they would write or the businesses they would open after the war. Some thought of heaven and hoped to get right with God before their time expired. Others simply dreamed of dying with dignity. They sought to meet their end on their own terms.

Humble hopes and dreams for the future kept these men alive. They made the choice to believe that there would be an end to their suffering. They lived for a brighter tomorrow; they held fast to a better story.

The power of a better narrative is incredible. It was the one thing that the Nazis couldn't take away from them. Life in the death camps proved "that everything can be taken from man but one thing: the last of human freedoms—to choose one's attitude in a given set of circumstances, to choose one's own way."[5]

While some agreed with the narrative of their experience —one that told them to give up and die—others stood firm in the belief that life would get better one day. No amount of evil could force them to give up their choice to live from a better story. They held fast to a narrative that brought meaning to their suffering.

Frankl found that, no matter what happens to us, we always have the power to choose the way we will respond. The right to choose our story is something that no one can take away.

It is amazing, isn't it? Admittedly, it feels like we don't have a choice. It's hard not to feel discouraged in the face of tough challenges. Anger and frustration swell every time trouble comes our way. Then the devil chimes in, spreading lies that our lives are hopeless, that we are alone, and that things will never change.

Yet, Viktor Frankl saw firsthand how people still had the power to choose their attitude despite all the Nazis threw at them. If there was ever a place to test whether hope could prevail, it was at Auschwitz, but even that incredible evil couldn't steal a person's right to choose their own story.

Remember, no matter what the devil may throw at you, he can't take away your power to choose your own story.

A Better Story

Recently, I sat in a church service and listened to a man tell his testimony. It was a story of his own brokenness and how God had rescued him. It was a gut-wrenching, funny, scary, uplifting, and tragic tale.

One part of his story was heartbreaking. He shared how he lost his baby daughter a few years earlier. She was born with a heart defect, and died only a few minutes after her delivery.

No one would blame him for being bitter. No one would fault him for having a bone to pick with God about it.

Yet, as he shared his testimony with us, there was no trace of bitterness or grief about him. He must have worked through that already. Instead of pain, his eyes were alive with joy. He had a sparkle, a shine about him. Instead of telling the story of his loss, his entire being radiated gratitude.

He talked about the joy of holding his daughter. About how privileged he felt to be there with her from the beginning to the end of her brief life. He shared how he felt a connection to her immediately. He felt a bond take place between them, and a peace as she passed. It was a sacred moment. He knew God was with him in it.

He lived from that story; from the story of hope and life amid death and loss. He cherished the brief moments he held his baby girl. He treasured what he received and made peace with what he had lost.

He stood firm on the truth that he would one day see his daughter again; that she wasn't gone forever. One day they would meet again, reunited for eternity. Until then, he would treasure the brief moments they shared deep in his heart.

He wouldn't dwell on what was stolen. Instead of living from the loss, he focused on the gift. He lived from the conviction that God gave him a priceless gift in the midst of terrible tragedy. Instead of bitterness over her being born with a heart defect, he brimmed with gratitude for the few moments of bonding they shared. He treasured the time he had to cuddle his beautiful baby girl.

He chose to live from a better story. He lived from a story of blessing, rather than loss.

I was stunned, I can't imagine what the loss felt like. My heart went out to him. I was amazed to see how he had made peace with her passing. It was a holy thing to behold the transformation of his grief into gratitude. Blessing, not loss, defined his story.

Living a Better Story

I want to live a better story. I want that for me, and I want that for you. I want you to come alive, to radiate the life inside you.

God made you a glorious person, a being filled with purpose, passion, and power. He made you for eternity. He made you to shine.

I know that your life hasn't been fair either. I know that this war hasn't been easy. I am sure you have suffered. Perhaps you've lost someone as well.

Whatever the past has been like, you can still live a brighter future. While you may not be able to change the past (though Jesus may want to reframe it for you), you can still choose how you respond to the cards life has dealt. You can always choose which story you are going to believe.

While the devil can do a lot, he can't defeat your spirit. No battle, no trial, no challenge you face can diminish your eternal identity. No evil can conquer the power of Christ within you.

You can choose how to meet the challenges you face. You can choose your story. Will you live a story of desolation, depression, and defeat? Or will you live a story of victory? The past doesn't define you. Your sin doesn't define you. The devil doesn't define you. Your identity in Christ is what defines you.

Live with gratitude and hope, even during your battles. God is by your side. His power is alive in you. You will have moments of great triumph. Amazing victories. There are breakthroughs coming your way. You will win the day.

Life isn't merely just battles, or heartache. It is fully of glory, beauty, joy, and wonder. Life is an adventure; don't forget it. Don't let the devil distract you from all the good already present in your life.

Savor joy. Choose hope. Fight the good fight. Even if you stumble, give yourself grace and get back in the fight as soon as you can. "The lovers of God may suffer adversity and stumble seven times, but they will continue to rise over and over again" (Prov. 24:16 TPT). You may have to fight the same battle a few times before you triumph. But you will triumph.

You were created to be a conqueror (Rom. 8:37), you are destined for victory!

Final Victory

Our ultimate victory is assured.

It may feel delayed. It will be opposed. At times, it may feel as if we are losing this fight. Sometimes, as Anderson points out "the reality of sin and the presence of evil may seem more real than the reality and presence of God."[6] But that is part of the devil's deception. In truth, darkness "is a defeated foe, and we are in Christ the eternal victor."[7]

The dark night and the fog of war always pass. Darkness always gives way to the dawn. So it is with us. The light of our Savior will break through the darkness. The glory of goodness will vanquish evil, once and for all. No more fighting. No more trouble. No more death or loss. No more crying and mourning. No more pain.

There will be a glorious celebration at the end of the war; a marriage feast to show the cosmos that the conflict is finally over. The Hero returned from battle, come to wed His beloved (Rev. 19). Happily ever after will have finally come. Heaven on Earth, at last!

Even as you wait for it, you can still enjoy peace. Inner peace is possible even as the storms rage. No matter what happens from this point on, you are still victorious. No matter what life may bring, you can overcome through the power of Christ within you.

Even the greatest threat—death—has no lasting hold. Death lost its sting when Christ conquered death (1 Cor. 15:55-57). The worst the world can throw at you is but a passing thought when compared to eternal bliss. Your never-ending joy is a truer thing than any evil you presently face.

Darkness will one day pass. You, in contrast, will shine forever!

Frederick Buechner reminds us that no matter what comes our way, we emerge victorious in the light of a new dawn.

> The worst isn't the last thing about the world. It's the next to the last thing. The last thing is the best. It's the power from on high that comes down into the world, that wells up from the rock-bottom worst of the world like a hidden spring. Can you believe it? The last, best thing is the laughing deep in the hearts of the saints, sometimes our [own] hearts even. Yes. You are terribly loved and forgiven. Yes. You are healed. All is well.[8]

Yes, the last thing about this world truly is the best thing. In the end, power will descend from on high. God will set the world right. You will spend forever loved, forgiven, healed, and free. All will be well, forever.

You will live for all eternity in glorious victory!

SEVEN

Your Story & My Final Thoughts

One of the marks of spiritual maturity is the confidence to resist the enemy with the authority of Christ—indeed, to be confident that that authority is effective against the host of hell.

Timothy Warner

Fight the good fight of the faith! Cling to the eternal life you were called to.

1 Timothy 6:12 VOICE

As we have seen, stories are powerful. Stories can entertain us. They can empower us. Or they can enslave us.

The stories that we believe will determine how we live our lives. Spiritual warfare is a war of propaganda—a battle to convince you to believe a lying narrative.

So, let me ask you the question again. *"Whose story do you want to believe?"*

It is time to let go of the old narratives that have held you down. It is time to uncover the truth about who you are. It is time to discover the story God is speaking about your life.

It is a simple process, though not always an easy one. You will need help to walk it out—we all do.

First, don't assume that just because your life has always been like this, or because you have always been a certain way, that things have to stay the same. Your past doesn't define your future—only God does. Redemption, and Christ's resurrection power mean that you can begin a new life right now.

Second, ask God to tell you the truth about your life. Ask Him how He sees you. Pray that He reveals the things He has planned for your life. Then, take some time and try to listen. It's good to give the Lord some time to respond when you ask Him a question.

Then, when He does respond, dare to believe Him. Trust Him. Trust that He knows you and that He sees the real you.

Often Christians dismiss God's voice because it sounds too kind. They become accustomed to the damaging dialogue inside their mind, and they assume it is true. Then, when the voice of the Lord speaks kindly to them, they dismiss it as wishful thinking.

But our God is kind. It is His kindness that brings genuine change (Rom. 2:4). The condemning voice of the enemy only robs our strength to keep trying. Listening to God's voice is the path to empowerment. So, learn to trust Him. Trust that what He says about you is the truth.

It may be risky. It may mean that you have to abandon things of the past. It may mean breaking ties with unhealthy relationships. It may mean making bold decisions for your future.

Faith means risk. It means that we put our convictions to the test. We have to decide how we will live. Either we listen to the story the Lord is telling, or we listen to the condemnation of the devil. We can't serve two masters. We can't live with two identities. It is one or the other. You have to choose. Either God can be trusted, or He can't. Either God speaks the truth, or He doesn't. Pick which one you want to believe.

Our greatest battle is the fight to believe that God's words are true. In the face of this, we must endeavor to believe the story God is telling in our lives. It is a glorious story that is bigger and brighter than any wounds we have suffered.

So, take the risk. It's time for you to dare to shine.

Fellow Freedom Fighters

As I said, you are going to need help to walk through the process of restoration. We all do. People were never meant to do life alone (Gen. 2:18).

We all need help to find freedom. The devil's lies are so pervasive, and we have already agreed with so many of them. So, we need help from others who can speak God's truth into our lives.

I realize this is may be a sore spot for many of us. Most of our wounds—and the toxic narratives we struggle against—came through other people. It may feel like it would be easier to just stay guarded and try to do this on your own.

I know it can be so tempting to put up walls, to stay defensive, and not trust others again. Yet, just as people have a lot of power to wound us, they also have tremendous power to help us heal. Often, we need others to be a part of the process. Some wounds only heal in healthy connection with other people.

Talk with someone who cares about you yet is still objective enough to tell you the truth. Seek out someone who sees your identity as something different than your problems. You need a confidant mature enough in their faith to recognize your story, and how it fits into the larger story that God is telling. This person also needs to have enough experience in spiritual warfare to recognize the lies that have hindered you.

If you already have someone like that in your life—a friend, mentor, pastor, spiritual director, etc.—bring them a copy of this book and tell them how it has affected you. Get the conversation started and talk about what is stirring in your soul.

If you don't know someone you feel you can talk to, you may need to do a little searching. Many great ministries exist to help people fight spiritual warfare and gain inner healing.

Yes, there are some other ministers and ministries out there that aren't so great. Sadly, the subject of spiritual warfare often has some unreliable voices speaking into it. When you are looking for someone to talk to about spiritual warfare, make sure they have read at least one book in the Recommended Reading or the Bibliography section of this book.

It is also important to recognize how you feel when you talk to someone. Do they make you afraid? Are they encouraging? Do they come from a place of condemnation or acceptance in Christ? Having a sense of comfort when you are with your advisor is key to accelerating your success.

Sadly, many ministers have done a lot of harm when it comes to spiritual warfare. They forget that their fight is with the enemy, not with the people they serve. They are the ones who enter ministry brash, brazen, and ready for battle. They brandish their swords and attack people with the Word of God. They end up wounding the very people they are supposed to help.

Stay away from those types and avoid anybody who seems like they have something to prove. Instead, find yourself someone who understands the journey. Look for others who have had to fight for their own freedom. Seek fellow freedom fighters—people who know what is like to reclaim their story.

You may have to get the ball rolling. You may have to be the one to initiate. Even so, God won't leave you to do this on your own. As you move forward, He will guide you toward those who can help you.

He will also guide you to others who you can help. You already have so much you can offer others. Another suggestion is to band together with friends and create your own group of freedom fighters. Share your stories with them. Allow them to speak affirmation and destiny into your life. Help them discover the truth about their own stories. Your experience—your story—has the power to help them. Your story is worth sharing.

Share with these people the truth about who you are. Share with them the truth about who God has made them. Let your light shine before others. Let others find inspiration in hearing the experience, strength, and hope you found on the frontlines of spiritual warfare. This is a key component in recovering your life from the influence of the enemy.

In God's hands, your story has the power to change someone else's life. With it, you can avert disaster and misery for countless others. Don't be afraid to generously share the freedom you have already found.

Final Thoughts

I hope by now you are more aware of the warfare you already face, and that you feel more equipped to handle it effectively. I pray you can one day declare, as the Apostle Paul did, "the Lord will rescue me from every evil deed, and will bring me safely to His heavenly kingdom" (2 Tim. 4:18).

No matter what attacks may come your way, the Spirit of God is always with you. He will guide you. Cultivate a greater conscious awareness of His presence within you, learn to hear His voice, and follow His lead. He will surely lead you to victory.

When the light finally breaks over the battle scene, we Christians alone will be left standing. It will be the people of God celebrating triumphantly as the last enemy falls. Until that day, let us keep fighting the good fight of faith. A crown of glory awaits us; a medal to memorialize our commitment to God (James 1:12).

So, dig in your heels. Stay steadfast. Practice a holy obstinacy. Take your thoughts captive. Choose truth. Listen to the story that God is telling about your life. And above all, dare to believe it!

Dare to own your identity. Dare to step into your authority in Christ. Command evil out of your life and spread the light of God into your sphere of influence. Be brave and, "let your light shine before others" (Matt. 5: 16).

The devil is hell-bent on robbing you of your identity. Evil will stop at nothing to convince you that you are nothing and trick you into settling for a lesser story. Satan wants to keep you playing small. Yet, you are much more than just a sinner saved by grace. Jesus rescued you from the "dominion of darkness" and brought you "into the kingdom" of Christ for all eternity (Col. 1:13). You are now a citizen of heaven (Philip. 3:20)!

You are a wonderful and powerful child of God, created to conquer. You were born to overcome. Stand firm in your faith. Stand firm in the story that God is telling.

Live from your identity in Christ, and you will live an amazing life!

BONUS RESOURCES

Reflection Questions

1. *Which stories in this book did you relate to? Why?*

2. *What toxic narratives have wounded your heart? What stories still plague you?*

3. *What have you missed out on in life by believing the enemy's lies?*

4. *What area(s) of your life need a better story? What narratives do you need to let go of?*

5. *Do you believe that God has a better story in mind for you?*

6. *When God looks beyond your sins and shortcomings, what do you think He sees?*

7. *What is your eternal identity? Who are you really?*

"My Story"

Are you living in alignment with God's story or does your life need a new narrative? Use this exercise to help you review and redefine your story. Ask God to reveal to you the story He is telling in your life, and finish the following sentences.

"My Story" Exercise

1. In the beginning, my life was:
2. There was goodness present when:
3. Then, this happened:
4. Afterward, I was:
5. And my biggest challenge was:
6. Jesus met me when:
7. God began my restoration through:
8. Now He is doing:
9. And I feel:
10. My happy ending is:
11. **My story is about:**

God's Voice

This is a quick guide to help you discern God's voice from the other voices we often hear.

Attributes of God's Voice

- Gentle
- Kind
- Loving
- Peaceful
- Encouraging
- Accepting
- Honoring
- Uplifting
- Inspiring
- Tells you that you are loved, wanted, and special
- Calls you holy, righteous, and redeemed
- When convicting you of sin, He tells you specific actions to make amends
- Lifts you up and draws you nearer to God, others, and your true self

NOT God's Voice

This could be the enemy's voice, messages from the world, or your own inner dialogue.

NOT Attributes of God's Voice

- Harsh
- Mocking
- Accusing
- Fearful
- Discouraging
- Rejecting
- Disrespectful
- Shaming
- Condemning
- Calls you unloved, unwanted, and unworthy
- Calls you unholy, disgusting, and damned
- Condemns with a blanket guilt, as though everything is wrong, and you can't overcome it
- Puts you down and isolates you from God, others, and even from your own heart.

Exorcising Ungodly Beliefs

Here is an exercise I like to take my clients through. It's a simple way to identify and eliminate the toxic narratives that sabotage us so we can expel those ungodly beliefs from our lives. Follow the steps below and use them as prompts to help you start a dialogue with God.

There is no way to get this exercise wrong. Just treat this time as a prayerful experiment; ask God to guide your thoughts, then see what comes to your mind.

1. Prayerfully ask God to show you the thoughts that are causing you distress today.
2. Ask Jesus to reveal the lie/toxic narrative that is behind these troublesome thoughts.
3. Ask God to tell you what He says is true.
4. Ask yourself, *"Am I ready to exchange this ungodly idea for God's truth?"*

When ready, say a quick prayer in which you exchange the lie for God's truth. The words don't have to be fancy, they just have to come from your heart.

Twenty Powerful Bible Verses to Take into Battle

The Word of God is a formidable weapon in spiritual warfare. Here are twenty powerful Bible verses for you to meditate on. Recite the verses out loud. Commit them to memory. Call upon them when trouble comes.

Deuteronomy 31:6 VOICE Be strong and brave, and don't tremble in fear of them, because the Eternal your God is going with you. He'll never fail you or abandon you!

Joshua 1:9 Be strong and courageous. Do not be afraid; do not be discouraged, for the Lord your God will be with you wherever you go.
Nehemiah 8:10 The joy of the Lord is your strength.

Psalm 23:4 Even though I walk through the darkest valley, I will fear no evil, for you are with me; your rod and your staff, they comfort me.

Psalm 27:1 The Lord is my light and my salvation—whom shall I fear? The Lord is the stronghold of my life—of whom shall I be afraid?

Psalm 27:14 Wait for the Lord; be strong and take heart and wait for the Lord.

Psalm 34:14 Turn from evil and do good; seek peace and pursue it.

Psalm 35:1 Contend, LORD, with those who contend with me; fight against those who fight against me.

Psalm 46:1-2 God is our refuge and strength, an ever-present help in trouble.

Psalm 91:2 I will say of the Lord, "He is my refuge and my fortress, my God, in whom I trust."

Romans 8:1 Therefore, there is now no condemnation for those who are in Christ Jesus.

Romans 8:15 The Spirit you received does not make you slaves, so that you live in fear again; rather, the Spirit you received brought about your adoption to sonship.

Romans 13:12 The night is nearly over; the day is almost here. So let us put aside the deeds of darkness and put on the armor of light.

1 Corinthians 10:13 No temptation has overtaken you except what is common to mankind. And God is faithful; he will not let you be tempted beyond what you can bear. But when you are tempted, he will also provide a way out so that you can endure it.

Ephesians 6:11 Put on the full armor of God, so that you can take your stand against the devil's schemes.

Philippians 4:13 I can do all this through him who gives me strength.

Colossians 1:13 For he has rescued us from the dominion of darkness and brought us into the kingdom of the Son he loves.

2 Thessalonians 3:3 But the Lord is faithful, and he will strengthen you and protect you from the evil one.

James 4:7 Submit yourselves, then, to God. Resist the devil, and he will flee from you.

1 John 4:4 You, dear children, are from God and have overcome them, because the one who is in you is greater than the one who is in the world.

Recommended Reading

These books, presented alphabetically, were instrumental in shaping my understanding of spiritual warfare. They are great resources that can add more spiritual weapons to your own arsenal. Enjoy!

3 Crucial Questions about Spiritual Warfare, Clinton E. Arnold.

Through his research and firsthand experience, Arnold tackles three big questions: 1) What is spiritual warfare, 2) Can a Christian be demon-possessed, and 3) Are we called to engage territorial spirits?

Spiritual Warfare: Victory over the Powers of this Dark World, Timothy M. Warner.

A simple, practical, easy-to-read, biblical, and reliable book on spiritual warfare.

Supernatural: What the Bible Teaches About the Unseen World and Why it Matters, by Michael S. Heiser.

An engaging biblical perspective on what the invisible world around us is really like.

The Bondage Breaker, by Neil T. Anderson.

This is a fantastic book with practical steps on how to find freedom from spiritual oppression. Anderson wrote several books on the subject, and all of them are worth reading.

The Great Divorce, C. S. Lewis.

A modern parable about the fundamental differences and the inevitable divide between good and evil, heaven and hell.

The Screwtape Letters, C. S. Lewis.

Eerily insightful fiction that peers into the realm of spiritual warfare and brings the tactics of our enemy to light.

Upper Dogs: Christians Have The Advantage. It's Time To Take It, Sarah Thiessen and Heather Hughes.

We Christians were never meant to live as the underdog. Rather, "In every moment, every situation, every relationship, every idea or possibility, we have the upper hand."

Waking the Dead: The Secret to a Heart Fully Alive, John Eldredge.

This is my favorite book on the subject of spiritual warfare. It is a wake-up call to see and engage the spiritual realm, and to choose to live a life truly worth living.

———

For current links to these and other great resources check out
www.vectorministries.org/resources

Share Your War Story

What's your war story?

If you have a story about overcoming a toxic narrative, or about how spiritual warfare has affected your life, I would love to hear it.

You can share your war story on the Vector Ministries Facebook page.

Or email your story to WarStories@VectorMinistries.org

References

1. The Devil & Fly-Fishing

1. Sarah Thiessen and Heather Hughes, *UpperDogs: Christians Have the Advantage. It's Time to Take It*, 54.
2. John Eldredge, *Waking the Dead: The Secret to a Heart Fully Alive*, 156.
3. Alcoholics Anonymous, *A.A. Preamble*, AA.org.

2. Orphaned Hearts & the Original Lie

1. Sally Lloyd-Jones, *The Jesus Storybook Bible*, 30.
2. Ibid.
3. Charles F. Stanley, *When the Enemy Strikes: The Keys to Winning Your Spiritual Battles*, 47, Kindle.
4. Edward Murphy, *The Handbook for Spiritual Warfare*, 439.
5. Ibid.

3. Unholy Agreements & Damaging Inner Dialogues

1. Peter J. Horrobin, *Healing through Deliverance, volume 2: The Practice of Deliverance Ministry*, 66.
2. Neil T. Anderson, *The Bondage Breaker*, 152.
3. Ibid.
4. Joyce Meyer, *Battlefield of the Mind*, 8.
5. John Eldredge, *Waking the Dead*, 159.

4. God's Truth & Your Identity

1. Neil T. Anderson, *The Bondage Breaker* (2000), 23.
2. Timothy Warner, *Spiritual Warfare: Victory over the Powers of This Dark World*, 12.
3. C. S. Lewis, *The Weight of Glory and Other Addresses*, Location 182, Kindle.
4. Graham Cooke, *Qualities of a Spiritual Warrior*, 7.

5. Your Authority & The Armor of God

1. Mark Bubeck, *The Adversary: The Christian Versus Demonic Activity*, 122.
2. John Eldredge, *Waking the Dead*, 162.
3. Clinton E. Arnold, *3 Crucial Questions about Spiritual Warfare*, 105.
4. Neil T. Anderson, *The Bondage Breaker* (1993), 42.
5. Aiden Wilson Tozer, *Born After Midnight*, 52.
6. Lincoln, Andrew T., *Ephesians*, Word Biblical Commentary, vol 42, 442-3.

6. Experiencing Trouble & Living in Victory

1. Sharon Beekman and Peter G. Bolt, *Silencing Satan: Handbook of Biblical Demonology*, 118.
2. Viktor E. Frankl, *Man's Search for Meaning*, 29.
3. Ibid, 36.
4. Ibid, 76.
5. Ibid, 66.
6. Neil Anderson, *Winning Spiritual Warfare*, 21.
7. Ibid.
8. Frederick Buechner, *The Final Beast*, 175.

Bibliography

Alcoholics Anonymous. "A.A. Preamble," AA.org.

Anderson, Neil T. *The Bondage Breaker.* Eugene, OR: Harvest House, 1993.

Anderson, Neil T. *The Bondage Breaker.* Eugene, OR: Harvest House, 2000.

Anderson, Neil. *Winning Spiritual Warfare.* Eugene, OR: Harvest House, 1990.

Arnold, Clinton E. *3 Crucial Questions about Spiritual Warfare.* Grand Rapids, MI: Baker Academic, 1997.

Beekman, Sharon and Peter G. Bolt. *Silencing Satan: Handbook of Biblical Demonology.* Eugene, OR: Wipf & Stock, 2012.

Bubeck, Mark I. *The Adversary: The Christian Versus Demonic Activity.* Chicago, IL: Moody Press, 1975.

Buechner, Frederick. *The Final Beast.* San Francisco, CA: Harper & Row, 1965.

Cooke, Graham. *Qualities of a Spiritual Warrior.* Vancouver, WA: Brilliant Book House, 2013.

Eldredge, John. *Waking the Dead: The Secret to a Heart Fully Alive.* Nashville, TN: Thomas Nelson, 2016. Kindle.

Frankl, Viktor E. *Man's Search for Meaning.* Boston, MA: Beacon Press, 2006.

Horrobin, Peter J. *Healing through Deliverance, volume 2: The Practice of Deliverance Ministry.* Kent, TN: Sovereign Word Ltd, 2003.

Lewis, C. S. *The Weight of Glory and Other Addresses.* Kindle.

Lincoln, Andrew T. *Ephesians.* Word Biblical Commentary, vol 42. Dallas, TX: Word Books, 1990.

Lloyd-Jones, Sally. *The Jesus Storybook Bible.* Grand Rapids, MI: Zondervan, 2007.

Meyer, Joyce. *Battlefield of the Mind: Winning the Battle in Your Mind.* New York, NY: FaithWords, 1995.

Meyer, Joyce. *Let God Fight Your Battles: Being Peaceful in the Storm.* New York, NY: FaithWords, 2015. Kindle.

Murphy, Edward. *The Handbook for Spiritual Warfare.* Nashville, TN: Thomas Nelson, 1992.

Stanley, Charles F. *When the Enemy Strikes: The Keys to Winning Your Spiritual Battles.* Nashville, TN: Thomas Nelson, 2004. Kindle.

Thiessen, Sarah and Heather Hughes. *UpperDogs: Christians Have the Advantage. It's Time to Take It.* Bloomington, IN: Westbow Press, 2015.

Tozer, Aiden Wilson. *Born After Midnight.* Chicago, IL: Moody Publishers, 1959.

Warner, Timothy. *Spiritual Warfare: Victory over the Powers of This Dark World.* Wheaton, IL: Crossway Books, 1991.

Acknowledgments

I thank God for the ability to write this book. Thank you, Jesus, that you redeemed me from a story of death and brought me into new life.

Also, thank you to my wife, Emily. Without your help and encouragement, I never would have been able to finish this project.

David created an awesome cover. Michelle and Darci did some great editing. Thank you!

I appreciate my fantastic in-laws and all of their support. Jeff, Dana, Becca, and Nicholas, you helped make this book a reality. Thank you so much.

Beth, Jenni, Shelley, and Steve, I value your friendship and counsel so much. Thank you, Carlo, Eric, and Howard for your encouragement and kind reviews.

So many friends and clients have encouraged me to write. Some of you have even given financially to make this possible. Thank you all!

And, thank you reader—without people like you who took the time to read this book, none of this would have possible. Thank you, and may God bless you and keep you always.

About the Author

Patrick Meyers is a Spiritual Director & Spiritual Transformation Coach. He holds two master's degrees from Denver Theological Seminary, and was ordained for ministry by BridgeWay Ministries International.

Along with his wife, Emily, he founded Vector Ministries to help other Christians find guidance to process through, and overcome, the kinds of issues they can't usually talk about in Sunday morning church.

Having survived many spiritual battles himself, he now shares his experience, strength, and hope with others, so they too can recover the life that God dreams for them.

As an avid angler, and father to three lively boys, Patrick loves being in nature and is committed to enjoying God's goodness in creation.

About Vector Ministries

Christians need more than Sunday sermons. They need to connect with someone who can help them navigate walking with God in real life.

Vector Ministries creates spiritual guide books and offers 1-on-1 spiritual direction to help Christians process their real-life experiences, overcome their struggles, and grow in a meaningful relationship with God.

For more information about Vector Ministries or about spiritual warfare, go to www.VectorMinistries.org.

VECTOR

Spiritual Direction & Transformation

Thank You for Reading

Thank you for reading *War Stories*!

If you enjoyed this book, please leave a review.

Reviews like yours can help other people find this book, and find freedom from the enemy's toxic narratives.

This is a self-published labor of love. Sometimes typos or formatting issues can slip through. If you noticed any of these, would you please let me know? You can email me at WarStories@VectorMinistries.org.

If you want to read more of my writing, check out my blog. I also have several new e-books in the works.
Go to www.vectorministries.org to learn more.

Made in USA - Kendallville, IN
1235748_9781736216309
02.17.2021 1312